Lunar Flower Priestess

Lunar Flower

Priestess

Ritual Magic & Healing Wisdom for the
Sacred Feminine Spirit

HANNAH CORBETT

In dedication and service to the Goddess within.

CONTENTS

INTRODUCTION

*L*unar *Flower Priestess* was written for women seeking the Goddess within. It is a guide to the practical workings of Divine Feminine Consciousness, meant to empower the Reader's Inner Priestess as a living manifestation of the Goddess. This how-to manual shows how you can use ritual magic to cultivate your best life and heal existing wounds. For tens of millennia, billions of women around the world have used magic for this very purpose. Only recently have we forgotten- or rather *think* we have forgotten- how to tap into this part of ourselves. Thankfully these ancient memories are encoded in our very bodies. *Lunar Flower Priestess* will show you how to take possession of this spiritual knowing and reclaim your latent powers, your sacred domain. You need only remember the language of magic, trust in your great power of discernment and intuition, then apply it with intention to your own life. This manual will guide you, not by dictating a formula or a prescription, but by furnishing specific reminders. You already know what you can do. These words are here to help you remember.

We each have our own magic, capable of healing our own bodies and spirits. My magic works because it is prescribed by me. Only I am in my own body, in my own world. The true, intimate and exact contents of this world are known only to me. Of this domain, I am the one true authority. In my own body, filled with my own spirit, filling my own world, I have powers unmeasurable and divine. You too, embody these mystical healing abilities, and need only to reawaken to your own sovereignty.

Alchemical practices such as Lunar Consciousness, Goddess Consciousness, and Plant Consciousness will be explored. By cultivating these powerful layers of spirit, you ascend into the legacy of Mystical Femininity, acquiring a deeper sense of connection, enhanced clarity, agency, purpose, creativity, intuition, and healing ability. Supported and guided by the Divine Feminine within, you are invited to experience the wholeness and unification of your physical and spiritual being. *Lunar Flower Priestess* is a map to the ancient pathways connecting our bodies, our Earth and the realms of spirit.

In the following chapters we will embark upon a transformational sacred-feminine journey. Please begin the process from wherever you are today, and enjoy what speaks to you in the now. Let your powerful intuition, good taste, and discernment guide you. Allow what feels most loving to you at any given moment to lead you to your own wisdom, healing and fulfillment. Trust in your direct connection to the Divine and cultivate a non-judgmental, openhearted approach to your spirituality and femininity. Be free and have faith. Feel the Tree of Life within you root down and hold firm as you reach for the moon and stars above.

Lunar Flower Priestess encompasses a number of initiations, expansions and integrations, allowing body, mind, and spirit to flow in a divine harmony. Come my Spirit Sister, walk this path of discovery, for it leads to a mystical garden. The gate is open. Inside the Moon Goddess beckons you to enter into her realm of sacred flowering.

PART I

BLESSED INITIATE

CHAPTER ONE
⸻Goddess ⸻Consciousness

You are the earthly embodiment of the Goddess, as is every woman's heritage. Yours is an inviolate spirit upon a terrestrial flight; meant to be cherished, protected and nurtured by the Great Mother. As you intentionally merge with her, she will bless you beyond your wildest dreams. Stepping into the power of Goddess Consciousness is a gradual process. Let yourself flow into her goodness. Open to her, and she will alight inside the altar of your soul.

Living Goddess

The very first step of Goddess Consciousness is to treat yourself as a Goddess. By honoring yourself, you honor her. In time, you might take it a step further, treating every female as a Goddess, including pets. At first, however, focus on yourself. Do something nice for your Goddess self each and every day. You might like to plant some new flowers, go dancing, take a walk in nature with your best friend, cook up a storm in your kitchen, practice martial arts, do yoga at home, meditate, or enjoy a relaxing bath followed by crawling into bed with a good book. Simply ask yourself what it is that feels nice to you, at this moment. Speak lovingly to yourself. Be kind to yourself, to the earth, and to those around you, in thought and in deed. Wear Goddess worthy clothing. Feed yourself healthy Goddess food.

Spend some time thinking about what embodying the Goddess means to you—what her adornments and home look like and how her power feels. Visualize your Goddess lifestyle. Ask yourself what is most pleasing to the Goddess within, and then take the necessary steps toward fulfillment. Amplify your manifesting power by asking for her assistance in materializing your Goddess path, and trust that her energy will reveal itself. Look for the signals that she sends you. She comes in through dreams, visions, elemental messengers, angels, answered prayers, signs and symbols.

Those committed to building a strong connection with the Goddess must regularly find their way into nature to experience the bliss of feeling at one with her. It is imperative that we feel the earth beneath our feet, the wind in our hair, and the warm sun on our backs. Nature reminds us of our own potential for healing, creativity, beauty and abundance. We require our walks in the forest, our mountain hikes, and immersions in rivers, oceans and natural hot springs, so as to be grateful for Mother Nature and to remember our own true essence, for we are of Her.

Earth Consciousness

The earth is our mother. She holds us and provides for us. We connect to her with our bodies, our senses and our love. We can do simple things for the environment to instantly deepen our earth connection. Picking up trash on your regular hike, detoxing your home and body of chemicals, or standing up against nuclear power in your community strengthens your relationship to the Green One. There are many tangible and practical ways that we can tap into a sense of oneness with Mother Earth. By planting a garden or simply going into nature we open ourselves to her. One can walk down a peaceful deserted beach and feel her quiet presence. Marveling at her perfectly tumbled stones, her soft sand and cleansing waters, it's easy to sense her there. Ideally, we can build up our connection to her until it's so strong that we can feel it at all times, in every environment, under any circumstance, because we are never truly separate from her. She is always there, within.

Even in the hustle and bustle of the city, you will find her. Look for her in the light and the dark, the shadows on the wall. She is in the tree down the block and in the sky above. She is in the moon's reflection in an oily alleyway puddle. She is in the marble column and each and every brick. She is in the women all around you. Cherish her in every drop of rain. Send love and gratitude to her for the spring blossoms. Open your arms and receive her fullness and perfection within your Goddess heart.

Maiden, Mother, Crone

The Triple Goddess appears in countless ancient pantheons and symbolizes the Goddess powers within each woman. She consists of the Maiden, Mother and Crone Goddess aspects all contained within us and reflected in the cycles of the Moon. The Maiden is associated with the waxing moon, the Mother with the Full Moon and the Crone with the Waning or Dark Moon. No matter what phase of life we are in, we are born with the wisdom of the Triple Goddess as a part of our spiritual DNA. Our journey to the Goddess is a matter of unlocking that wisdom, power and self-love. She teaches us that every part of the cycle is sacred, including death. The continuity itself is sacred; every ending is just a beginning.

Goddess Consciousness is multidimensional. As we move through the seasons of life we come to know her many forms. She offers up different aspects of herself to help us value and understand the undulations of the cycle. We in turn, step into our greatest potential by celebrating her natural rhythms; flowing, becoming, reaping and replenishing. We do nothing alone. She supports us in all we do. If we can surrender to her current, she bears us along to greater shores than we could ever imagine. Listen deep within for her wisdom. Identify the quiet Goddess whispering below the chatter. Tune in to her voice. Turn up the volume, for She is a part of you, the most important part.

Life in this Goddess garden is a divine gift. She invited us here to her green world. We journeyed here to blossom and grow, to love with these tender hearts, to sense and taste all she has to offer. We seek her bliss without attachment. We celebrate her cyclic nature within our wombs, the seasons, the turning of the wheel. We take solace in the familiar smells of autumn as we gracefully let go of the sweetly fading summer. Our positive attitude towards life, our embodiment of rhythmic Nature, our inner Goddess glow; these are the simple secrets that fill us with her magic.

The Mariposa Grove

Yosemite National Park is home to a magical grove of Giant Sequoias. For an entire century, forest fires were carefully suppressed in order to preserve these ancient beings. Yet, in all that time there were no seedlings, because as it turns out, fire is required to release the seeds from the pinecone. Fire is also necessary to clear the brush on the ground, and to open up the canopy above. The ash creates a fertile ground for growth, and the openings in the canopy allow the sun to reach the seedlings. Meanwhile the mature Giant Sequoias have a thick fire-resistant bark which protects them through a blaze. In this expression of the Divine Feminine, destruction is understood as an important step in the greater cycle of creation. In the Mariposa Grove there is no life without death. There is no birth without sacrifice. All of Nature joyfully offers herself to this mystical and passionate dance with fire. I once was there in the Mariposa Grove. I walked amongst the Tree Elders and knelt in wonder at the feet of the Creatrix, contemplating the fiery birth of every Giant Sequoia, feeling the immensity of their gentle and mysterious spirits.

Goddess Invocation

By calling the Goddess into our rituals we honor her and regain some of her wisdom. Whichever Goddess speaks to you at any moment of your life is the right one. The more you think about her, learn about her, dream of her, the more powerful you both become. Ambrosia, the food of the Gods, comes from us. Our worship is ambrosia. Our love feeds and sustains the Divine. When a Goddess is obscured and no longer worshipped, we can imagine her fading away. Thusly, we can imagine that recovering her from obscurity, feeding her the nectar and ambrosia of our love and devotion, will make her and us strong again. Allow yourself to be interested in a Goddess. She can come from any culture and any time. Feed her bits of ambrosia and soon she will be filling you just as you fill her. The moon is the purview of many a Goddess, as is the earth- seek one who speaks gently and kindly to you.

Goddess Altar

Build an altar to the Goddess of your choice. If you are not sure which Goddess you would like to honor, you might find one who resonates listed in the Goddess Compendium below. Or you can simply devote your altar to The Goddess, the one source of all that is. In this ritual please allow yourself to open to your own natural creativity and intuition. Spend some time thinking about Her and familiarizing yourself with her symbols, her gifts, her powers. Then go about gathering your materials.

Plan what, where, when and how. Your plan can be meticulous and methodical or it can be totally spontaneous- however you wish it to be! Let your inspiration take over. You could go into nature and build an eco-safe altar with found objects. You could create a little space in your home to dedicate to the Goddess Altar. You might want to make your altar small or large, simple or elaborate, hidden or for all to see. It could take minutes, hours or days to build your Goddess Altar.

Bring whatever energy you have available at the moment to this practice and allow yourself to enter the altered consciousness of devotional altar building. As you build, pray to Her, make offerings to Her, feed Her, honor Her and love Her.

Goddess Compendium

Here is a small collection of Goddess lore. It is my belief that all Goddesses are of one source. No matter what culture, place or time she comes from, no matter what name she is called by, her root essence is of the one source: the unchanging, pure soul of the Divine Feminine, the one that has always been and will always be.

Asherah- Semitic Mother Goddess, also known as Queen of Heaven, Lady of the Sea, Creatrix of the Gods. She was Yahweh's consort and co-creator. Asherah poles were worshipped in temples next to Yahweh's altar and upon high hills with tree groves on them. She is not only associated with the sacred tree but is often depicted as one. She is the tree of life. Her other symbols are the serpent and the lion. She is in the water, the stars and the trees. She represents abundance, nurture, love, kindness, sensual nature, fertility, creativity and protection. Appropriate offerings: grapes, dates, wine, pomegranates, cakes and walnuts

Inanna/ Ishtar and Ereshkigal– Mesopotamian Goddess of love, sex and war. Worshipped through sacred prostitution. Queen of Heaven. Associated with Venus, the morning star and evening star. Her symbols are the lion, the tree, the owl and the serpent. Between Ishtar and her sister Ereshkigal, the Queen of the Underworld, the two sisters represent the dark and light aspects of nature. Ishtar presides over the harvest, the full moon, healing waters, pleasure, freedom, independent women and the Female Power principle. Her tree is the Huluppu. Appropriate offerings: pomegranate, grains, lotus seeds, wine, cake

Lilith- It is said she was Adam's first wife, formed out of mud, the same as him. Lilith could not bear his constant need to dominate her sexually. She wanted out of the garden. Rumor has it, she left him to go procreate with a bunch of demons along the shores of the Red Sea. She sprouted wings, said God's name and flew out of the garden. Since Adam couldn't handle a woman of his equal God decided to make him a new wife out of Adam's own rib. This new wife would be more subservient, they hoped. Lilith embodies independent, free-thinking and indomitable woman-nature. Some people say she is the serpent that later slithered into the garden to tempt Eve into knowing. Lilith asks us to honor our instincts and desires, to be strong, bold and true. Lilith does not settle nor subvert her nature. She tastes the fruit of life. Appropriate offerings: wine, blood, tree fruit

Wadjet- Egypt's "Green One". Depicted as a Green Cobra or as the Left Eye of the moon. She lives in the Milky Way. Or perhaps, in her Serpentine form she *is* the Milky Way. She embodies healing, rebirth, fluidity and wisdom. She imparts magic, medicine, protection, revelation and psychic intuition. She is also associated with Bast, sometimes appearing as dual-form lion-headed Wadjet-Bast. Her colors are turquoise and emerald. Appropriate offerings: red clover, serpentine, turquoise beads

Sekhmet-Bast- Dual-form Egyptian Goddess. Sekhmet is the Lion-headed Warrior Goddess. As Sekhmet she embodies Divine wrath. She is the punisher and destroyer aspect of the Divine Feminine. As Bast she embodies the more playful, benign, sensual and domestic qualities of a Feline. Bast is the protectress of hearth and home, the embodiment of the Temple Guardian. Appropriate offerings: blood, ale, pomegranate, song and dance

Nut- Egyptian Goddess of the Night Sky. Mother of Isis and Osiris. Wife of Geb, Father Earth. She is depicted as midnight blue with stars all over her body, which arches over the earth, her husband. Her breasts rain nourishment upon the earth below. She gives birth to the sun each morning. Appropriate offerings: milk, flowers, harvest grains, sage

Isis- Egyptian Mother Goddess. Daughter of Nut, Mother Sky and Geb, Father Earth. Sister-wife of Osiris. Mother of Horus. Mother of Magic. Queen of the Dead. Isis offers compassion, protection and prosperity. Her colors are turquoise and emerald green. Appropriate offerings: ale, wine, water, cedar, figs, dates

Yemaya- Mother Goddess originally of the Yoruban Aborisha faith. She migrated across the Atlantic with the African Diaspora and traveled the new world with her people. She is worshipped in Voudou and Santeria among other Orisha traditions of the Diaspora. Yemaya birthed the Earth, Moon and Sun. She is known by many names and is worshipped as an Ocean Goddess and Mother of All Waters. Patroness of Fishermen, she originally hailed from the River Ogun. Her name translates as "Mother Whose Children are Fishes". She is Goddess of fertility and women's health. Her colors are blue and white. Appropriate offerings: mother of pearl, silver coins, shells, coconut, coffee beans, moon stone

Hel- Norse Goddess of the underworld. Her name translates as "hidden". A Giantess. Half her body appears beautiful and alive. The other half is decaying flesh and bone. She represents the dark and light aspects within ourselves and life itself. She represents the wholeness of the cycle of life, death and rebirth. While Viking warriors who died in battle went to Valhalla, Hel's underworld is reserved for those who die of disease or other natural causes. She decides who will be born again. Hel aids with astral journeying, communing with the dead, and divination. Her colors are black and white or blue. Animals associated with Hel are the wolf, the serpent, the hound, the owl, the eagle and raven. Appropriate offerings: black and white cookie, apples, stones, bones, earth, blood, dried flowers

Kali- The Dark Goddess aspect of Devi. She is Time the Destroyer. The embodiment of the destructive aspect of the sacred feminine. In her path of chaos and death are sown the seeds of renewal, just as the dawn follows the darkest night. Kali asks us to trust and surrender to her flow even through changes and loss. She helps us to cut away and burn that which no longer serves. Her animals are the tiger and the elephant. Appropriate offerings: red roses, menstrual blood, red wine, red rice, lotus flower and seeds, dance, fire

Pele- Hawaiian Volcano Goddess of Kilauea. Creatrix/ Destroyer. Volatile and passionate. She can be both loving and punishing. Even in her wrathful aspect she is creative, for her lava flows and cools creating the island for her people to live on while her ash creates fertile ground for new growth to nourish and sustain her devotees. Appropriate offerings: Aloha (respect, peace, compassion and kindness), local flowers and fruit

Spider Grandmother- Native American Creatrix, especially prominent among Pueblo traditions (Kokyangwuti is her Hopi name). She is the weaver of life. First she wove the stars and then she wove consciousness and the rest of creation. She sits in the center of all that is, all that she creates. She calls us to weave our own webs, to create our creations, to bring industriousness to fulfilling our purpose on earth. She reminds us that we are all connected within the web of life. We are never separate, but all one woven whole. Appropriate offerings: sweetgrass, hospitality, creativity, dew, thread, woven things

Corn Maiden- Native American Corn Goddess, whose legends abound across many nations. The corn is her sacred flesh. Her only wish is to feed all living beings. She is a teacher of gratitude and respect for the sacred earth. She calls us to follow her example, to lovingly and abundantly give of ourselves to nurture and protect the natural world all around us. Appropriate offerings: corn, corn meal, corn husk dollies, a living corn altar in your garden, compost, water, love and gratitude, earth stewardship

Pachamama- Incan Earth Mother Goddess. She is found in the earth below, in the mountains, the trees, the rivers and the rocks. She creates and sustains all life. She is in the abundant harvest and the fertile field. She aids with the fertility of all living things. Her nature is generous and loving but can also be punishing at times that humans disrupt her natural balance. Envisioned as a dragon that lives beneath the Andes, when awakened she expresses such volatility through earthquakes and volcanic eruptions which serve to rebalance the ecosystem over time through cycles of destruction. Pachamama is the living earth. The earth is the sacred flesh of the Goddess. She asks that all of humanity return to a natural and sacred way of life that honors her and restores the balance of the whole. Appropriate offerings: corn, beer, sweets, food prepared with love, environmental stewardship or activism, right-living, earth consciousness

Kuan Yin- Chinese Goddess beloved among many Buddhists across the world. Goddess of Compassion, Healing and Fertility. Kuan Yin hears all prayers. Virgin Goddess, Protectress of women. Appropriate offerings: rice, nectar, willow branch, lotus flower and seeds

Gaia- Greek Mother Earth. The Creatrix of the Universe, she formed herself out of Chaos. Then she created Uranos, Father Sky to cover her. Mother of Aphrodite. Grandmother of Selene. Gaia represents the Great Mother. She heals, loves, listens, nurtures and brings forth all. Appropriate offerings: stones, crystals, water, wine, seeds, roots, fire

Aphrodite- Greek Goddess of love and beauty. Daughter of Mother Earth, Gaia, and Father Sky, Uranos. Mother of Cupid. Born of the sea. Known as both the morning star and the evening star, she is Venus. Appropriate offerings: beach roses, gardenia, seashells, ocean water

Artemis- Greek Goddess of the forest, the hunt and wild animals. Maiden of the waxing moon. Her symbols are the stag, the She-bear, hunting dogs, the boar, bow and arrow, and her beautiful crescent moon crown. Artemis aids with animal communication and cleansing of the Self. Appropriate offerings: dog biscuits, mugwort, fresh berries, honey, cedar

Selene- Greek Mother Goddess of the Moon. Granddaughter of Gaia. Sister of the sun and the dawn. She also wears the crescent moon crown and is often depicted riding a chariot across the sky. Her familiars are the raven and the owl. Selene's purview is intuition, fertility, childbirth, the unconscious and miracles. Appropriate offerings: fresh white roses, pomegranate, seashells, water, sparkly things

Hecate- Thracian/ Greek Guardian of crossroads. Patroness of witches. A triple-form moon Goddess, most often associated with the dark moon aspect. A huntress, she travels with her dogs (Priestesses). She offers protection, magical assistance, wisdom. She guides the dead. Aids with divination and prophecy. Associated with the Willow tree. Appropriate offerings: Dandelion, Lavender, dog biscuits, cakes, seeds

Cailleach- Ancient pre-Celtic Winter Goddess. The Cailleach rules the wintry weather. She comes to life on Samhain when she goes about striking the earth with her wand, delivering frost into the ground. At the end of winter she turns back into a boulder which constantly exudes moisture. Her sacred plant is holly. She is protectress of animals and ruler of many natural elements such as water, stones, hills and caves. She is depicted as a veiled hag or a large bird carrying sticks for her hearth fire. Appropriate offerings: a corn husk dolly dressed in plaid woolens, sacred stones, holly boughs, fire wood, ale, bread and butter, water, milk, fish, seeds and eggs

Bloddeuwedd- Celtic Flower Goddess. Maiden Goddess of the earth, youth, blossoming and summer's fleeting nature. Daughter-in-law to Arianrhod, and created by the Moon Goddess' brothers out of oak leaf, primrose, cockle and meadowsweet, Bloddeuwedd was intended to marry the moon's son. As punishment for rejecting and betraying her husband, she was turned into an owl by his uncles. While she is associated with spring and summer, her transformation into a creature of the night symbolizes the ever changing seasons, cycles of light and dark, life and death. Appropriate offerings: oak leaves, fresh flowers, fresh berries, seeds

Arianrhod- Celtic Moon Goddess. Known as "The Silver Wheel Who Descends into the Sea". Mother Goddess and benevolent guide of the Dead.

11

Owl shape-shifter. Associated with the North Star, ivy plant, birch tree, wolves and spiders. Appropriate offerings: seashells, silver coins, sea salt, beach roses, moon stone

Cerridwen- Celtic Mountain Goddess often associated with the Crone. She is the keeper of sacred knowledge, wisdom, inspiration and good fortune. She presides over magic, fertility, harvest, death and rebirth. Her symbols are the divine cauldron, the sow and the crow. Appropriate offerings: herbs, harvest grains, acorns, sparkly objects

Baphomet, Mother of Blood- Ancient shadow aspect of Albion's Earth Goddess. Her essence connects all that is. She is the Giver and the Receiver of all blood. There is no life or death without her. She brings forth all, just as she consumes all. She exalts the beautiful cycle of continuity in life, death and rebirth. Her animal is a ewe or ram representing fertility and virility. This animal symbol speaks to the Goddess' deeply earthy element. Her voice issues forth from the earthen grave. She is guide to those who walk the left hand path. House cats are her messengers. The ultimate gatekeeper, she is known as both Earthgate and Stargate. She creates openings for souls to travel between realms. Appropriate offerings: dance, blood, water, wine, quartz crystals, the fertile womb

CHAPTER TWO
The Tree and the Serpent

T ree consciousness teaches us patience, stability and continuity, how to breathe, how to give forth and take in. Serpentine consciousness teaches movement, vitality, self-mastery and renewal. In this, our mystical garden, every flower, every weed, every fallen feather has its own special teaching for us to learn and grow from. From the cicadas suckling at the roots of the tree, up to the great horned owl roosting on the highest branch, the Goddess is there at every level, inspiring, comforting and illuminating. She is the tree of life, just as we are its embodiment. Long ago, before we learned the guilt and shame associated with the tree and the serpent, these symbols belonged to us. They were ours. If we learned to fear them, it only means that we learned to fear our own nature. It is of great healing significance for us to reclaim the sacred symbols of the Goddess as we reclaim her in ourselves.

These alchemical archetypes connect us to our inner divinity. It is the symbols of the Tree and the Serpent which will help us to remember our chthonic powers. The Goddess hovers just beyond the veil, beckoning from the past, and promising the future. The serpentine consciousness within you not only protects and heals your body, but also gives you herbal knowledge and healing abilities. This serpent is your spiritual link to the underworld, the root origin of life, death and rebirth. The snake is the source of your energy, your magic. As it rises upon the tree inside you, so does your power. Meanwhile, the tree grounds, purifies and uplifts your spirit. By embracing these layers of plant and animal consciousness you tap into a primal alchemical source, an essential nature deep within yourself.

Be this tree. Grow and root. Embrace this inwardly spiraling power serpent, as a part of you that has possibly been estranged, but now is coming home. It might seem alien, but it is a spiritual aspect which has been hidden like a treasure, within your own shadows.

Tree Hugger

This can be a simple gesture or a slightly more elaborate ritual. Either way, it is a grounding and releasing practice which will expand your tree consciousness. Tree energy is strong, gentle and loving, so give a big tree a good long hug, letting the weight of your whole body melt into the tree, especially at the solar plexus. Be aware of any heaviness you may have been carrying as it gathers to the solar plexus, leaves your body, and enters into the tree. The tree will take it down and put it into the earth to be transformed. At the same time the tree generously fills the new space inside you with a sense of peace and grounding.

Whenever you are ready for some energetic refinement, just locate the nearest big, strong tree and hug away. Or take a walk to visit your favorite local tree.

After you're done hugging the tree you might sit down in her roots for a while and feel into the earth below as you lean back into her trunk as the sun filters through her leaves bathing your eyes in soothing green light. If it's warm out, you could take your shoes off and put your toes into the dirt. Bring a water bottle and offer your tree friend a drink. Give loving thanks to the Tree Spirit.

Big Tree, Little People

A couple of years ago I was at a women's gathering in a ceremony with about twenty other women. The group was led by Liv Wheeler, a Shaman who spent eight years in Burkina Faso learning to channel the Kontomble and has since dedicated her life to traveling the world in ceremony to share the messages of these sacred nature spirits. The Kontomble are the Little People indigenous to every land on earth (also known as gnomes, leprechauns, faeries). They are our ancestors and the creators of all culture including but not limited to cuisine, music, dance and dress. In this particular ceremony we were gathered, sitting on the earth around a Grandmother redwood. Liv channeled the Little People who in turn delivered messages from the ancient tree.

This particular tree stood alone in a forest of different species of trees. All the other redwoods around her had been logged decades earlier, but she remained. The little people came through with much grief for the forest and the nearby ocean, for the whales. They asked us what was happening to the earth and why? It turned into a group of wailing women, all of us weeping for the earth. As I write these words my heart aches again and tears run down my cheeks in remembrance of this deep wound we carry for the violence against our planet, a grief we rarely allow ourselves to feel.

One of the women asked what we could do to help and how we could connect with the wisdom of the Little People. The message that came through was that first we could offer our tears and that then we should plant seeds. Simply getting in touch with how sad we are about what is happening to the earth is the first step. Through the offering of the tears we come into a place of truth and power. From there we can plant the seeds of change and renewal. The seeds are both symbolic and literal. By literally planting a seed you come into relationship with the natural order of things, taking your rightful place in the garden. By planting a seed you affirm and empower the supremacy of healing and creative principles.

15

In gratitude to the Little People, to Liv and to all the forces that gathered us under that tree to receive those truths I share this message with you. Have you ever pushed aside a dark feeling in witnessing the desecration of nature? I ask you now instead, to let the feeling come all the way in and let the tears flow.

It's okay to love your mother. It's okay to hurt for her. It is good and it is right. It will bring you to a place of power and action no matter how small that action is. Offer your tears. Plant your seeds. They are needed.

Wadjet

In a vision I saw an eye. It looked like the Eye of Horus but it was reversed- it was the left eye instead of the right. The eye had a shape inside the pupil like a crescent moon. As I discovered later, the ancient Egyptian Goddess Wadjet is known as the Left Eye of the Moon. She embodies the Lunar Feminine Principle. She inhabits the Milky Way, bestowing intuition, magic, healing, medicine, protection, revelation and transcendence. She is often depicted as a green cobra and is also known as "The Green One". She influences the third eye and crown chakras.

At the time I had the vision of the Left Eye I was lying on a table, my body covered in crystals. I was in my first session with Angel Healer, Shamanic Spirit Teacher and High Priestess, Nicole Hoegl. After our session Nicole told me that as she was clearing my subtle body, a huge serpentine guardian with emerald and turquoise encrusted skin rose up above me. The serpent told her that it had been with me since my birth and would protect me always.

Serpent Celebrant

How do you celebrate your serpentine consciousness? There are countless ways. Some of my personal favorites are: practicing yoga, wearing snake prints, dancing a serpentine dance, lying on a rock and soaking up the sun, wearing flat shoes (or going barefoot) so that I can feel connected to the earth below and draping myself in comfortable clothing so that I can bring consciousness into every part of my body the way I imagine a snake inhabits its body; fully and unencumbered. I nourish myself with the foods that most benefit my constitution. I celebrate my feminine body's own serpentine cycles of releasing and renewal with menstrual rituals.

I remember all of the times I've encountered the serpent in nature and how I felt in that moment- yes, sometimes fear - but always awe, always a sense of great mystery and revelation. I invite you to take a moment to contemplate the symbolism of the serpent: renewal, transformation, sensuality, medicine, earth energy, wisdom, healing, protection, wholeness, cosmic consciousness, awakening, Goddess energy, Gnosis.

As Above / So Below

Alchemical transformation occurs when we master ourselves as pure channels of Divine energy. Our earthly bodies are both receivers and conductors of all kinds of energy. Are you aware what frequency you are tuned into? Do you know how to work the dials of your psychic apparatus? What kind of energetic vibrations are you receiving- sound, light and emotion, for instance? Do you feel in tune or out of tune? Do you know how sensitive an instrument of reception you really are? Imagine your ability to change channels or to tune in very attentively to a particular energy. By mastering the receiver and conductor aspects of your subtle body, you can not only control what kind of frequencies you allow in and out, but you can also transform your energy through internal processes of alchemical refinement.

There is that which is above (God energy) and there is that which is below (Goddess energy) and we are the connectors in between. The grounding and nourishing powers of the earthen realm below are perfectly blended with the astral light of heaven above, within our corporeal channels. Our flesh bodies are the antennae of the living earth, receiving and transmitting divine love. We use the physical vessel to aid in the work of the spirit.

The flesh is to be purified in the Alchemist's fire. Through discipline the Spirit is liberated within its vessel. We require devotional practices to deliver us to that place of communion. As you become the Alchemist of your own spiritual destiny, you might layer different practices in your effort to tune your instrument and prepare your body and mind. There are many ways into the Goddess Temple. In yoga this concept is embodied in Kundalini rising. Kundalini energy lies sleeping, coiled in the root chakra at the base of the spine. Through posture, yogic breath and meditation, yoginis balance the two essences of the Divine Masculine (Shiva) and the Divine Feminine (Shakti) and remove energy blockages in the chakras (psychic centers of the subtle body), thus awakening and allowing the Kundalini to rise up through the chakras, releasing out of the crown in Divine Unity, as the energy cycles from earth to heaven and back again in an unending flow. This concept is represented as two serpents twining around the Tree of Life (the spine).

The idea of energy directed from within the sacred earth, transmuted through the Alchemist's vessel (the body) and liberated into the heavens where it cycles back down in an endless loop of love and light is about ecstatic self-mastery. It is the influence of mind over matter which allows transformation of the spirit. By tuning into and refining the Divine energies within, your channel is occupied by pure, uplifting love and light. The Tree of Life is inside of you. In cultivating the tree, your body becomes healthy, your mind becomes peaceful and your spirit becomes free.

Breath of Miracles

Sit with your spine straight- either on the edge of a chair with feet flat on the floor or on a floor mat in lotus pose. Slow and deepen your breath. Your body is a pure vibrating channel. All the fluids and minerals and ores inside your corporeal vessel are there to facilitate your alchemical function. As you send the roots of your sacral chakra down into the earth, the earth elements within your own blood are activated. The iron core of the earth, the secret subterranean mineral springs, the copper, the arsenic, the salts are all resonating within your blood, charging the energy within your channel.

With every inhale you feel that earthy metallic essence rise up into your tree like sap in the springtime. Continue moving this earth energy up through each chakra with each inhale. As this force rises it clears the chakras and frees up energy. As it reaches the crown of the head the energy gains momentum, releasing up and out into the heavens. Now you are receiving energy from both the earth and the heavens within your vessel. The inhale fills you with the earth's charge from below and each exhale brings a cascade of pure sparkling light from above, down through the channel of your body. Imagine that essence moving through you, above you and below you in an infinity loop.

Continue this breath for as long as is comfortable. When finished, take a moment to retract your roots and scan all your chakras to bring your energy back home.

I am She

I begin with the tree and I end with the tree.

I dream the tree. I am the tree.

I am the marriage of earth and sky.

Alchemy, inside of me.

I plant myself.

I grow. I root. I dig. I reach. I twist.

I dance in the sky.

I close my eyes, see two serpents kiss.

They climb upon the sacred tree that is me.

I am She.

I bleed life into earth below.

I give forth and I take in.

I am sap and I flow.

I am flowers.

I am fruit.

As high as I reach, so deep do I root.

I am shelter.

I am pathways.

As above, so below.

I forgive and I forget.

I am life and I am death.

I prophecy.

I am the tree.

I am She.

CHAPTER THREE
Lunar Consciousness

Lunar consciousness is one of the foundations of a magical life. It is another way of attuning with nature, by surrendering to the influence and cycles of the moon. By devoting yourself to the moon, life takes on a particular harmony. Lunar consciousness is as ancient as the moon herself. She has been there to guide you all along. She asks you to wax with her and to wane with her. Surrendering to her flow adds a dimension of ease and structure to earthly existence. Since animals, plants, our own pineal glands, our wombs and the earth itself are already completely under the sway of the moon, we naturally fall into a rhythmic flow with the world around us, by fully embracing lunar consciousness.

The cycle of the moon, begins with the new moon, followed by two weeks waxing to the full moon, followed by two weeks waning back again to the new moon (reborn). This cycle repeats thirteen times per year. Lunar consciousness teaches us to mirror the moon's cycle in our own waxing and waning. We do this through new moon and full moon rituals, in daily life practices, as well as through simple lunar awareness and appreciation.

Flow: Wax and Wane

Just as farmers plant their seeds on the new moon, so can you ritually plant the symbolic seeds of that which you wish to manifest in your life. These seeds of intention are planted on the new moon and over the next two weeks they sprout into fruition as the moon grows into her fullness. These two weeks of waxing are a time of attraction, action, forward motion, achievement, implementation, and reaping. As the Moon waxes to fullness, offer gratitude for that which you are manifesting in your life, and begin to contemplate the approaching time of waning.

The full moon and the following two weeks of waning comprise the time period for ritual releasing, cutting away and cleansing. In preparation for your full moon releasing ritual ask yourself which parts of yourself are no longer serving a purpose or are even holding you back from becoming your best self. Meditate on creating a ritual that will signify your intentions about letting go of that which is not essential or useful to your purpose in life. For the two weeks after your full moon ritual, while the moon wanes, you will be aware of the unburdening with which the moon aids you, as she herself appears to become smaller and smaller. In unity with her, she supports you as you let go. As she fades into the darkness of another new moon, so does the residue of that which you've released.

When the new moon returns you are reborn, prepared to process again around the moon wheel, ready to plant some new seeds. You have made room. You have pruned and cleared. The soil of your moon self is freshly turned, fertile and receptive to new growth. You have become the gardener of your own consciousness, reaping and sowing intention. Through practicing lunar consciousness you will know when to go inward and when to go outward. You'll know when to rest and when to work; when to begin new projects or finish old ones; when to laugh and play; when to retreat into a place of asylum. You'll know when to take care of yourself and when to take care of others. The more you develop lunar consciousness the clearer your own wisdom, intuition and self-expression become. Lunar consciousness is a foundation upon which other ways of being may be constructed. It is the vessel of a magical life. Here is a simple Moon Meditation you can perform anytime which will help you center into your moon consciousness.

Moon Meditation

Wearing comfortable clothes, come to a seated position in a quiet place. You can sit on the floor in lotus pose or kneel. Or you can sit on the edge of a chair with your feet flat on the ground and your spine straight and long but also supple and relaxed. Go slowly as you read the words. Once you get the feel for this simple breath, you will be able to close your eyes and go deeper.

Imagine you are a celestial body. Visualize the blood in your body as a vast salty ocean. Your breath is the moon which acts upon the tides of the ocean within you. Intentionally slow and deepen your breath. Exhaling, allow your chin to slowly drop towards your chest, keeping the spine long. Inhaling, lengthen the spine and lift the chin gently. Bring awareness to any tension in your shoulders as you soften into your breath.

On each inhale visualize the dark new moon waxing to fullness in synch with the fullness of the breath. Fill the lungs up to the very top until they are overflowing like the full moon. Pause at the top of that fullness and visualize that fat bright full moon within you. Then gently release the breath, as you visualize the waning of the moon; the three quarter moon, the half-moon, the crescent, smaller and smaller until you are completely empty of air and the moon too is void. Pause at the bottom of the exhale and hold the dark emptiness of the moon against the ocean's tide within you, before slowly inhaling again. When you have the hang of the visualization, repeat this moon breath nine times with your eyes closed.

Lunar Awareness

Lunar consciousness begins with a lunar phase calendar. Simply by tacking your lunar calendar to the wall, you take the first step into lunar consciousness. Now you will know what the moon is doing at all times. Now you will have access to the moon's secret life. You'll know how best to harmonize your own movements and efforts with hers.

Maybe at first you don't think about ritual practice or using the pull of the moon to support your own objectives. Perhaps in the beginning you just let the awareness of the cycle of the moon be there as your daily practice- just knowing if she's waxing or waning, when the new or full moon is coming. Maybe at first you just allow yourself to wonder at her rhythmic perfection and grace as you watch her wax and wane in the sky above. Eventually she will invite you to harness her mysterious powers for ritual practice.

When you are ready to experiment with lunar ritual, be spontaneous and intuitive. Trust that your intentions can not be lost in translation. When you plant your seeds, their meaning is clear. Your prayers are heard, undistorted. Let the objects and substances you use in your rituals reflect your intentions and resonate with whichever Goddess you are in devotion to. Let your rituals reflect your areas of interest, the texts you study, the seasons and places you find yourself in. You are in conversation with the Divine. You are in communion. Your intention is pure.

At times you might have an intense ritual that goes around the entire moon cycle, beginning as a releasing ritual and ending up as a manifesting ritual. Other times you might not be moved to perform a ritual at all but you will still be in tune with and aware of the movement of the moon. It could be because you are busy and short on time. Or it could be because the last ritual you did was so powerful it is still rippling through you, transforming your reality. Whatever the case may be, respect the ebb and flow of your own creative ritual energy.

Magical Moon

My earliest memory of the magical Moon is of traveling with her while driving in a car at night with my mother at the wheel. The full moon followed us everywhere we went. I basked in her benevolence and rapturous beauty. She mesmerized me with her soft mysterious light. Her magic was woven so thick around us that I could see it, luminous and golden. To this day, as much as I know about the moon, she is constantly surprising me. Appearing at the oddest moments. Moving in unknowable arcs. Still following me after all these years. She reminds me that I am her child, full of wonder and mystery divine.

Moon Walk

On the full moon, go for a walk with the moon. Maybe invite a Spirit Sister or two. Whether by yourself or with company, reflect on everything you know and don't know about the moon. Think about your earliest memories of the moon. Notice as you walk whether you are following Her or if She is following you. Turn towards Her and pause to feel her full light on your face, subtle and pure. Ponder her influence upon the earth, the oceans, the crops, your own psyche, your womb and the water within your body.

As you walk, identify one thing- a thought pattern, a behavior, an emotion or the like, which you want to release. Stand and face the moon. Cup your hands in front of your heart and imagine that thing in your hands. Extend them out to the moon, offering Her your burden.

Over the next two weeks allow the power of the waning moon to gently support your releasing intentions. As you continue upon your ceremonial walk, tap into a sense of gratitude, for all over the whole earth, the moon is guide to all who are willing to remember her sacred ways.

Lunar Rites, Sacred Hours

Moon days such as the New moon and the Full Moon are sacred. These are ideal times to move into ritual consciousness. The steps leading into ritual are important. The more steps we take, the deeper we go. First the bath washes away mundane thought patterns. Donning the robe or blessing the talisman are more symbolic steps deeper into the ritual. These are the outer edges of the proverbial labyrinth, the center being the height of the ritual's magic. It is the many little steps of the ritual that build into a powerful transformative force.

Waning Moon: Undoing

In the framework of Lunar Consciousness, what is so striking is the perfect balance of attracting and releasing. We spend most of our time thinking about what we want, how we're going to get it, the way we want things to be. But the moon teaches us that we must spend exactly half of our time and effort letting go and cutting away in order to create room for that which we wish to attract. Releasing rituals are performed on the Full Moon and over the following two weeks of waning.

You may have a lot of releasing to do. There may be quite a bit to clear away. This is joyful work because in the end, the space created will be filled with the dreams you wish to manifest. Imagine clearing out a wild untended plot of land in order to plant your perfect garden. You are both gardener and garden. You are the sower and the reaper of your own destiny.

As you develop your ritual practices you will have your own very personal, locational and seasonal reasons for the flowers and herbs you use; the crystals, the seeds, the fruit. As long as it makes sense to you, it will make sense to Her. Design your beautiful moon garden exactly as you wish.

Full Moon Releasing Ritual

This basic framework can come in handy for any full moon ritual at any time of the year. Fill in the particulars with elements relevant to your heritage, situation, season and location. By performing these rites you harness the power of the moon to create the future that you desire. The moon supports you in releasing all that no longer serves your greater purpose. As you focus in on that which you wish to let go of, the power of the waning moon clears the way for that which will be planted at the new moon. The more you release now, the more you can plant later.

Gather your thoughts and intentions regarding your releasing ceremony. Ask yourself what habits, objects, relationships or thought patterns you would like to be free of. Gather the elements that you've chosen to represent your intentions, to honor the season and whichever Goddess energy you are working with, such as: fresh or dried flowers / herbs, candles, seashells, cakes, ale, wine, fruit, grains, seeds, dirt, crystals, water, milk, honey

Prepare yourself with a ritual bath. Make up your own or try this releasing and purifying bath- Make an infusion with 6 cups boiled water and the following herbs: 1 tbsp Comfrey, 1/4 cup Lavender, 1/2 cup Nettles. Strain the infusion into your bath and enjoy. To add an extra layer of psychic cleansing add a half cup of sea salt to the bath. Be sure to hydrate and moisturize afterwards.

Smudge yourself with mugwort, sage or cedar. Dress up in finery intended to honor the Moon. Anoint yourself.

Write down on a small piece of paper all that you intend to release over the next two weeks as the moon fades to black. Meditate on these intentions until they are etched into your mind. These are intentions of that which you wish to release, cut away and let go of.

Go to your ritual space (outside ideally, but you can adapt this for indoors as well) and begin by invoking the Divine. Close your eyes and visualize

27

yourself within a channel of pure radiant moonlight. Cast a circle of Divine Protection using a sacred herbal tea or a bit of salt. Ask Goddess, God, Angels, Guardians and Guides to inspire, bless and protect your ritual space.

Build a little altar and make your offerings to the Moon. With hands in prayer, ask for her assistance in releasing and letting go. Burn the paper in a fire-safe vessel and scatter the cold ashes. Release the sacred circle by giving thanks and well wishes to the Divine Ones who held space and amplified your magic. Walk away without looking back.

Waxing Moon: Reap What You Sow

As you release, cleanse and purify, you are creating a lot of space inside for new things to grow. Once you have completed a cycle of releasing you are prepared to ritually materialize your dreams as the moon waxes, beginning at the New Moon.

Using the structure provided by the moon, build your manifesting and attracting rituals to flow with the waxing of the moon. As the New Moon waxes into fullness, your seeds of intention come to fruition.

Intention is the seed which the will germinates. Intention is the root from which the seedling grows. Intention becomes the fruit we reap as it is transmuted. When you are crystal clear and pure in your intent, you are articulating your vision and power and transmitting it. Alchemically that positive and purposeful energy goes out into the ether and returns to you in crystallized form.

New Moon Manifesting Ritual

Adapt this manifesting ritual framework to fit any purpose, season or place. It will allow you to harness the power of the waxing moon as you grow your intention to fruition.

Prepare yourself with a ritual bath. Make up your own or try this Blessing and Protection bath- Make an infusion with 6 cups boiled water and the following herbs: 1/2 cup mugwort, 1/2 cup roses, 2 sprigs of rosemary. Strain the infusion into your bath and enjoy.

Smudge yourself with herbs. Dress up in finery intended to honor the Moon.

Meditate on your seeds of intention until they are etched into your mind. These are intentions of that which you wish to manifest, grow, become and invite in.

Write your intentions on a small piece of paper. Place some symbolic seeds (anything from your kitchen cabinet will do- sesame, chia, celery, cardamom) on the paper and fold it into a small seed packet.

Go to your ritual space outside in nature and begin by invoking the light. Ask your Angels, Guardians and Guides to protect and bless your ritual space. Dig a hole in the ground and plant your symbolic seed packet in the earth. Pour some water over your symbolic planting as you ask the Goddess to bless your seeds of intention and assist your progress. Give thanks and close the circle. As the moon grows into her fullness over the next two weeks, your intentions will take root and grow as well.

The Moon and Stars

As the moon orbits earth, she travels through the twelve signs of the zodiac. It takes her about two days to move through each sign. At every single new moon, the moon and sun are in synch within the same sign of the zodiac. If, let's say, the sun has moved into the sign of Aries on March 21, then you can be sure the next new moon will be "New Moon in Aries". Then two weeks after that, when the moon is full, and is half way through her journey around the zodiac, it will be "Full Moon in Libra" as Libra is the sign opposite Aries in the zodiac. The next new moon will be in Taurus followed by a full moon in Scorpio which is the sign opposite Taurus in the zodiac. You don't need to keep track of these precise movements in order to perform your ritual magic, but you may develop an interest in these details over time.

As you go deeper into your lunar consciousness you might enjoy getting into the nuances of the moon's movement within the greater astrological aspects, and also relating the placement of the moon to your own natal chart. For example, when I was born, the moon was in Scorpio. This means my moon sign is Scorpio. It has been my experience that whenever the moon returns to Scorpio (whether new, full or somewhere in between) I feel most intimately aware of her. It is a feeling of home-coming.

CHAPTER FOUR

Cosmic Consciousness:
The Universal Dance

On a globe that spins around a burning star, we orbit and we are orbited. We inhabitants of Goddess form, we dance a universal dance. We sing the galactic song. There is no easier way to access the Goddess than by simply synching with her rhythms. We find our natural place in her divine clockworks. We take our meaning from her sacred geometries, her looping satellites and her perfect cosmic compositions. The moon's rhythm, the sun's rhythm, the earth's rhythm, the stars' and planets' rhythms- these are our guides.

Child of the Sun

In many ways we instinctively practice solar consciousness. We sleep at night when we are turned towards the night sky and we wake during the day when we face the radiant sun. Depending where we are on earth in relation to the sun, we celebrate the local seasons as they mark our yearly orbit. We sing songs about the sun, bow to it and bathe in its light. We eat food that grows from the earth because of the sun's energy. The sun's light is that of the Creator, the Divine Impregnator. Our sun is generous, ever so potent, loving and warm. We receive each and every sparkling new day as a gift, wrapped in the godly light of the rising sun. Every aspect of life on our feminine earth is dependent upon this sacred masculine source.

It is possible to distinctly experience the perfect balance of cosmic consciousness by going into nature and disconnecting from artificial light and sound. At sunset each day you would begin getting ready for bed. The gently falling dusk would lull you to sleep. If the moon were full she might wake you with her light in the middle of the night. You might get up and crawl out of your tent for a cosmic star and moon bath. But then you'd go back to sleep until dawn when the birds would wake you with their song for the rising sun. Have you ever experienced how sweet it is to live in this rhythm? If not, I highly recommend getting yourself some camping gear and adventuring into the woods, the desert or the mountains! Journey into nature, into yourself, into connection, balance and restoration.

It truly is soothing and deeply centering to simply embrace the natural cycles of darkness and light. Go and lay your head down, far from the sounds of motors, sirens, alarms; far from street lights and glowing screens. Slow down to the real pace of nature. Find your stillness on the forest floor. Cosmic consciousness is a harmony of solar consciousness, stellar consciousness, lunar consciousness blended perfectly with the grounded earth consciousness that comes with sleeping directly upon the earth, hearing only the sounds of the forest, breathing the fresh air and being among the trees and all the other flora and fauna. All your senses are cleansed and refined in the kindness of the natural world.

Whether in the woods or at home, I do my best to keep that slow and connected feeling alive. My bedroom is an electronic free zone. I usually go to sleep early and I love getting up with the birds. Sometimes as dusk is falling I purposely leave all the lights off, just sitting and watching the sunlight fade and the darkness grow. Then I remember the feeling of being in sync with nature; quiet, balanced and peaceful. The earth, sun and moon all teach us to flow with grace, to do and undo with the universal rhythms, leading us back to our own true nature.

Sun Dance

Stand (barefoot on the earth, weather permitting) with your feet together and face the sun. Breathe deeply. Soften your knees. Shift your hips from side to side subtly. Roll your shoulders up and back, allowing your arms to hang. Breathe. Shift your tailbone forward and back, finding a comfortable place for your spine to rise from, like a tree. Let each deep full inhale emphasize the upward reaching motion of your tree. Each exhale emphasizes the downward rooting force of the tree. Your legs are roots shooting down, seeking the center of the earth. Feel through the bottom of your feet. Sense the connection to the earth, the Great Mother. Seek her through your rooting toes. Being mindful of the breath, allow the energy coming up from the earth to move through your feet and legs, gaining momentum, rising into your tree trunk. Let that power grow through you, animating your branches, as your arms gently rise into the sky seeking the light of the sun. Allow your elbows and wrists to spiral and your fingers to undulate like leaves dancing in the breeze. Let the breath energize your supple tree dance.

Gently looking up with your eyes while keeping the neck long, raise your arms above the head, clasping hands and flipping the palms up to the sky, stretch up and feel the strength and flexibility of your tree. Gently and softly twist towards the left. Come back to center. Gently and softly twist towards the right. Come back to center. Inhaling, reach up again and ever so slightly back for a gentle back-bend, while keeping the tail tucked and the front body flexed and strong, bottom ribs pulled in.

Bask in the glorious sunlight and bow with gratitude, clasping your hands, palms together, arms above your head, core flexed and tailbone tucked as you slowly bend forward from the hip and let your torso hang.

Unclasp your hands, with knees soft, chin and tailbone tucked, slowly roll up to stand, head coming up last.

Again raise your arms, float your hands out into the sky as branches extending from your heart. Breathe and make the smallest undulations throughout your tree, dancing in the sun. Bring your hands into prayer. Take a moment to give thanks for the Earth below you, the Sun above you, the life inside you and all around you.

The Wheel of Return

Ancients used the wheel to represent the idea of life in time, spinning round and round, moving ever forward, yet always returning back again just like the earth in its orbit of the sun. Equinoxes and solstices are marked in the Wheel of the Year to celebrate the earth's relationship to the sun and the changing seasons therein.

The equinoxes and solstices delineate the four quarters within the wheel. Within each quarter is a midpoint which is considered the high point of the essence of that season. Each of these eight days are sacred within the wheel of the year and are perfect times to celebrate and honor the Nature Spirits. These are the most potent days of the year to gather, to build altars, to make offerings and connect with your place in time on earth.

Where you live has everything to do with which symbols you associate with the seasons and their corresponding celebrations. Tailor your festivities to the seasons as they occur in your part of the world. Especially celebrate that which is unique to the season as it relates to your land, your culture and your personal relationship to nature.

Observe the many little signs that tell you a new season is marching across your threshold. Savor each flavor of the season as it passes by. Ponder what seasonal celebrations are most important to you and practice them with intention and gratitude, as a way of connecting with your place in nature and time.

Spring

On the equinox the length of the night and the day are equal as Mother Nature awakens. Now the long sunny days will overtake the cold dark nights of winter. Everything is new as the Wheel of the Year turns again. Here in the Northeast the snow melts. The thawing earth gives forth a cold perfume. The crocus and daffodil emerge and bloom. The forsythia as well. The magnolia and cherry trees will soon bud and blossom, the dogwood and lilac. All of nature comes alive, bursting forth. The eggs are in the nest. The sap is rising in the tree. Soon enough the peonies will blossom. The Spring Equinox brings the promise of rebirth, lengthening days, warmth and abundant new growth. We celebrate the season by building altars to the waking Goddess, by going forth into nature and getting mud on our boots. We decorate eggs and hang them in trees. We gather by the fire with loved ones to feast and celebrate. We rejoice that the long winter is behind us. Another cycle of death and regeneration is complete and we ourselves are reborn as well. We plan our gardens with eager anticipation. We are ready to spring forth into the green season ahead. My favorite spring rituals are making dandelion wine with my mom, harvesting nettles for making soup and planting seeds in the garden. *Offerings for the Goddess in Spring: Eggs, daffodils, crocus, tulips, forsythia, rhubarb tart, fire, water, nettle soup, fiddleheads, seeds, bulbs*

Summer

As spring's parade of flowering trees gives way, the longest day of the year has arrived- the Summer Solstice. Summer is here. The oceans and the rivers are warming up. The greenery is filling out. Nature is budding and blossoming all around. Gardens are sprouting forth and the seeds of hope are watered with care. The long dark winter is a distant memory, amidst the burgeoning vitality of summer. We ourselves are vital, strong, nourished by the sun, energized by the long bright days and the fresh abundant harvest. We build altars to give thanks for the fruits of the summer season. We harvest and dry our herbs, savor every trip to the ocean or lake and revel in our cool morning walks in the park. We dance under the moonlight in the warm summer breeze as the fireflies sparkle in the dark. We feel the nocturnal passion for life inside us as the summer peaks and the nights grow gradually longer. I love to walk down a cool dirt path barefoot, to a secret swimming hole. I like to sit under a tree and listen to the cricket song. In summer, I feel the energy of the Corn Maiden grow strong as the corn grows tall. Around the first harvest, which is the midsummer holiday I make offerings of corn every day to the beautiful, nurturing and gener-ous Corn Maiden. *Offerings for the Goddess in Summer: corn, roses, daisies, watermelon, raspberries, blackberries, lavender, corn husk dollies, fire, water, ale, seashells, drift wood, mint, dandelion wine, elder flower*

Fall

As summer climaxes and recedes we are urged towards the coming autumn. There is something crisp and electric in the cooling air. The har-vest is underway. On the Equinox the day and night are again of equal length, but now the lengthening nights will overtake the quickening days of autumn. It is time for reaping and gathering; time to celebrate the season's bounty which will carry us through the long winter ahead. We take stock in this moment, grateful for the abundant earth, the bountiful harvest, the sacred hunt. We are sustained and in the turning point of this season we feel the vitality of the living earth, even as she descends into a period of dormancy. We feel her pulsate within us, as the elements within the earth reverberate through our blood. We are connected as Nature settles into her quiet rhythm. We dance her autumnal dance. In the fall I want to climb a mountain, to walk through an orchard or a vineyard during the harvest. I love the sweet smell of autumn leaves as they dry in the sun. My favorite fall ritual is simply to build an altar out of nature's bounty, featuring the season's harvest, honoring the cycle of death that is so beautifully enacted as the green world changes color. *Offerings for the Goddess in fall: asters, figs, pears, persimmons, grapes, squash, bittersweet, acorns, oak leaves, sweet grass, chrysanthemums, wine, fire*

Winter

The bear is in her cave. The squirrels have gathered their winter stores and grown fat. The numerous juvenile hawks, still learning to hunt, will now face their first winter and likely their last. Only a small percentage will survive. This is winter; cold, stark and beautiful. We embrace this season as a time of inward journeying. We find a quiet place inside ourselves where we are grateful for the dormant winter, the time of repose. By adapting to the stillness of the season, winter becomes a time of replenishment and retreat. The Winter Solstice celebrates the shortest day of the year, because after this long night the days will gradually grow longer. Even though the coldest days are ahead, the darkest days are behind us. We rejoice and exalt the strange beauty that is winter, so very different from all other seasons, so mysterious, sparkly and bright. My favorite thing about winter is the quiet. I like to snowshoe in the silent woods, the creaking of branches and the crunch of snow underfoot as the only sound. The sun shines bright off the pristine snow and I am at home in nature. I love to cook nourishing soups in winter, to stay near my hearth fire. I often feel like the bear in her cave, dreaming, resting and replenishing. Winter is a lovely time for reflection and self-care rituals. *Offerings for the Goddess in winter: chestnuts, seeds and grains, winter squash, pomegranate, elderberry cordial, holly and evergreen boughs, candles, fire*

The Cailleach

On the eve of Imbolc, which is the mid-winter holiday, I had three vivid bird dreams. In the first dream a flock of bird people landed on the ground next to a river outside my window. It was winter and the trees were bare. The bird people's bodies were humanoid, wrapped in woolen blankets, patterned in white with red and black. They moved like birds and their faces were unfathomable masks. They traveled with a white falcon with red and black markings. The bird people had two small orphans in their care, dressed in blue and white striped pajamas.

In the second dream I was riding on a train next to a marsh. A great blue heron landed there in slow motion. The sun was low in the sky and lit up the heron's feathers in a most spectacular fashion. The bird was electric blue with neon pink highlights. I pointed this out to the other passengers but they didn't seem to notice.

In the third dream I was on top of a snow covered hill where people were sledding. Then the snow was gone and the weather became pleasant and my mom was there with me. A gigantic bird of unknown species came down from the sky to land on an old stone wall with a holly bush next to it. My mom and I went very close to the bird even though it was visibly aggressive.

The next day I was researching the history of Imbolc and came upon the legends of the Cailleach, a Goddess I'd never heard of. In the many legends I came across there were elements from all three of my dreams, such as: winter, rivers, stones, marshes, hills, herons, giant birds, orphans, plaids (patterned woolens), and holly.

The Cailleach is an ancient pre-Celtic goddess of winter. She is sometimes depicted as a giant bird. She spends spring through fall in the form of a damp boulder. Then at the time of Samhain (the mid-autumn holiday) she takes the form of a hag who goes about striking frost into the earth with her wand.

At the time of Imbolc, halfway through winter, the Cailleach, who controls the winter weather would make sure to have a bright sunny day so that she could go out and collect enough firewood to last out an extra-long winter. If on the other hand she was asleep and forgot, then the weather on Imbolc would be dark and unpleasant, but she would run out of firewood and then winter would soon be over.

This year Imbolc was a clear sunny day and the Cailleach was very much awake in my dreams. She must have been out there collecting her firewood because we did in fact have a long cold winter.

Four Quarters Vision Mapping Ritual

At the time of each equinox and solstice there is a moment of gathering-perfect for long term plans and dreaming of the season ahead, all the potential, all the seeds to be planted, all the flowers that will grow and the bountiful harvests our plans will yield. This vision map ritual is a manifesting practice that is one part to-do list, one part prayer and one part magic. You may wish to repeat this practice seasonally at every solstice and equinox.

You will need a notebook, a pen, colorful markers or watercolors, some glitter perhaps and a large heavy weight sheet of paper. First take some notes on your most important goals and dreams for the season ahead. Get clear on your intentions and break down big ideas into smaller steps. Be specific about the details associated with these goals and dreams.

Now move to your large sheet of paper. Draw a star at the top and write the word Manifest in the center, color the star with vibrant hues. Maybe add some glitter. Now start mapping out your intentions in words and pictures. Create symbolic containers for the goals to fill. You are creating space for your dreams to come into reality. These symbolic containers are boxes for you to check, bubbles for you to fill in, blank spaces for you to write in results. Say you want to plant ten new rose bushes- draw a rose and write "plant roses" then draw ten blank check boxes around the rose that you can check off as you actually plant them. Say you also want to make three new friends- draw a heart and draw three blank horizontal lines inside it, write "make new friends" above it. As these friendships manifest, fill in the names of your new friends on the blank lines. Say you want to do a big project- break the big idea down into smaller steps and map those out on the page with corresponding empty spaces to be filled in with the completion of each step.

Have fun and be creative with your vision map. Hang it on your wall where you'll see it often. Feel free to add to it as increasing clarity around your intentions flows to you.

The Four Sacred Elements

Earth, Wind, Fire and Water are the four elements of our Cosmic Consciousness and of our natural world. Each of these elements balances the others. Depending what is going on in your birth chart it may be more or less challenging to maintain harmony between these elemental forces in your world. This is one of the ways Astrology can be helpful in understanding yourself. In my chart for example, there is a lot of fire, a lot of water, a little bit of air and a very tiny bit of earth. This means I spend a lot of energy consciously working on grounding and keeping my fire and water in balance. I imagine if I was born with a lot of earth, then I would feel grounded most of the time. I wasn't born that way, so I have to work on it every day.

Inviting balance between the elements is something you can do by cultivating a relationship with each element. In your altars you can make sure to always have each element represented in one way or another. In your daily life you can connect with gratitude to the elements that bring you nourishment and enhance your energy flow. Check in with the four elements each day and develop a personal awareness of what both balance and imbalance feel like. Use this awareness to know what is needed within you, on an elemental level. Think of yourself as a flower. You need all of the elements to grow and thrive, but neither too much nor too little of each. You need just enough sun, just the right amount of water, just the right composition of soil and just the right quality and quantity of air. When all is in balance, you can grow and blossom and spread your seeds.

Balance and Blossom Ritual

Build a small circular altar. Place a flower in the center representing you, a lit candle in the south representing fire, a cup of water in the west representing water, a stone in the north representing earth and a feather in the east representing air. Take your journal and a pen and dedicate one page to each element. Sit for a while and write some of your favorite personal stories and ancestral mythologies about each element. Celebrate your place at the center of the natural elemental world.

Fire- I remember being three or four years old, when our next door neighbor's house burned down in the middle of the night. We woke up and went outside to watch it burn. I thought it was the most glorious sight I had ever seen. Afterwards my mom made me a cup of chamomile tea with honey and milk.

This summer I was watching my Aunt Nina (whose birth chart is dominated by fire) tend to a fire pit in the middle of a field. The charred logs in the fire made the shape of a large skull. To me it looked like the Lord of Fire was laughing. Whenever Nina would add something to the fire, flames would shoot out of the skull's mouth and sparks would fly out of his eye sockets. I realized then that Nina is a Fire Priestess.

Water- When my mother learned to swim, she was taught to ritually cup the water in her hands and speak to it. "Dank u water" she whispers in Dutch, before diving in. Her father did not believe in God, but he believed in water. He was descended from boat builders and lived in a land claimed

41

from the North Sea. His world was punctuated with reverence, gratitude and respect for water.

My other grandfather was descended from Portuguese fishermen. He was himself an amazing fisherman and taught all his progeny to fish and boat. He was fearless on the ocean and took us on many wild adventures. We always felt safe out on the big magical ocean in a tiny boat with Grandpa. He had many protective water spirits all around him. The ocean was his mother. She fed us. She washed us. She held us and rocked us.

My mom baptized me in a pristine river gorge, when I was in my early twenties. It was quiet except for the wind in the trees. The water was dark and ice cold. She floated me on my back and used her hands to submerge me as she whispered her blessings over me.

Earth- My mother's birth chart has four planets and her sun in Capricorn. She is an earth mother in every sense- steadfast, hard-working, nurturing, creative and practical. She has the most beautiful garden in the world. She is my rock. She is all the earth I have ever needed.

My great-great grandmother was a Dowser or what you might call a Water Diviner, that is, one who uses a divining rod (a Y-shaped willow branch) to locate water underground. This tradition was passed down to my great-grandmother and then to my uncle. This story could be filed under water, earth or air, as it has to do with a connection to the earth, awareness of hollow ground, places where air and water spirits move within the earth.

When I was a child I had a killer cat and a cemetery for the small birds and rodents that she caught. While I was at it I also scraped up any roadkill from in front of the house and buried that in the cemetery. I knew that in the earth was where they belonged. As I've grown older I've retained this knowledge that the earth will take all things in need of transformation. I frequently lay my body upon the earth. The earth takes what is in need of transformation and pulls it from my body. It feels like a magnet, when it is happening. For a few moments my body is locked into an earth portal and then released when the exchange is finished.

Air- Learning how to breathe properly may be the single most impactful healing experience in my life. Learning how to shift consciousness through the breath, how to use respiration to process and move energy and emotion within the body, how to stay present within the air inhaled, learning to pay attention to the breath and the emotion it stirs- how much the breath had to teach me! Then practicing that breath, experiencing life through the breath, knowing that I can always find a place of truth through the breath- this brings me immense peace and power.

Spirit speaks to me through the birds. Birds are the messengers of Spirit, inhabitants of air, riders of the wind. They call me from on high and show me new perspectives. They remind me that the wheel is always turning in the winds of change and that my spirit truly is as free as the air. At first it was just the crows and ravens. As a teenager I dreamt of my father wrapping me in the embrace of a massive raven's wings. Then it was the raptors- I could write a whole book about the lessons I learned from the great horned owls in Golden Gate Park. The red-tailed and red-shouldered hawks are always with me. I once saw a murmuration of starlings make the shape of an eye in the sky- perfect and distinct- and then it was gone. I am in constant relationship to all the birds around me; listening, watching, paying attention.

CHAPTER FIVE

Ritual Consciousness:
Enter the Labyrinth

As we gradually expand our spiritual pathways and practices, ritual becomes a part of the everyday, elevating the mundane. Cleaning the house, or feeding the dog can become ritualized practices that serve to center us within, and connect us to the larger whole. By filling your days with practices that elevate the routine, you can live a life that celebrates every moment as a Divine gift. Life becomes ritual—one rite leading into the next, serving to bring gratitude and blessings to every aspect of earthly existence. This is pleasing to the Goddess.

There are many layers of this labyrinth, many secret gardens within. As you develop these inner realms, you come to know and trust yourself more completely and to feel more at home within your body and the space you occupy. By refining aspects of self, such as Heart, Body, Spirit and Mind you walk the path homeward, to embrace a sacred life. In this chapter we'll explore different practical methods of such refinement. You can layer these concepts and practices into the foundations of your ritual life.

Nine Goals

As the spiritual garden grows over time, you patiently fertilize the ground of perception, trim the hedges of thought, and cultivate the blossoming rose of consciousness. By adopting the following nine goals as guiding principles in everyday life, the garden easily springs forth around you. I encourage you to read this list often and intentionally plant these thought patterns in the soil of your own psyche. Take note of the ways you are already embodying these ideas. Also contemplate the areas of your life or in the world at large that could benefit from the further application of these principles. Adoption of these goals will guide you to the very heart of the Goddess Garden, the seat of your highest wisdom and most potent ritual magic.

- Know, love and heal yourself

- Express yourself and create your creations

- Live a sacred, pure and connected life

- Eat, breathe and move as the Living Goddess

- Center in gratitude, abundance and generosity

- Think, speak and do from the heart

- Flow with rhythmic nature

- Protect and honor the Earth

- Celebrate the Creatrix and her Mysteries

Gathering

Think of gathering as the first step of ritual consciousness- that moment when you gather your thoughts, your intentions, and your focus. You gather yourself into the center. You home in on what is needed, in your life and then for your ritual. During the gathering phase you bring order to your thoughts and your domain, clarity to your purpose. You go into the outer world and gather the objects needed for the ritual. You return home and wait for the moon. You clean house and make your preparations. When the time is right you commence with your procession ever deeper into the labyrinth.

The gathering is a time of great potential and creativity. You envision the ritual itself and the transformation it begets. Your cauldron awaits all the precious ingredients that will soon bubble and swirl with power and intention. There is a sense of purpose, anticipation and inspiration which animates the gathering. Soon you will invite your Spirit Allies into the circle, but for now you can feel them fluttering around the edges. You hear the whispers of the approaching honored guests. You imagine their cravings, their hungers and thirsts. You decide what offerings you will make, which prayers you will pray.

Purification

Bathing can be performed as a healing or cleansing ritual all its own or it can be done as a step in a larger ritual. It is highly appropriate to come to any ritual space physically and spiritually clean and as such ritual baths prepare body and mind for the work of the spirit.

Methods of detoxification and purification include steam bath, sauna, sweat lodge, natural hot springs or a simple homemade herbal bath or salt bath. In the US we have an abundance of natural hot springs which provide all manner of profound therapeutic benefits- physical, emotional and spiritual.

The oceans, rivers and lakes all around us also provide powerful ritual healing and purification opportunities. Just as Nature constantly cleanses and renews our waters, she purifies us as well.

At home you can use herbal infusions, decoctions, minerals, unpasteurized cider vinegar, essential oils, crystals and more in your baths. Magically, salt is known for its ability to absorb psychic energy and draw it back to the earth. You can use a blend of sea salt and Epsom salts for both psychic purification and physical benefits as well as customizing your herbal infusions to match your ritual intentions.

Protection Bath

Make an overnight infusion of 6 cups boiled water and the following herbs:

1/4 cup Burdock Root, 1/4 cup Chrysanthemum, 1/4 cup Mugwort. Strain the infusion into your bath and invoke the light.

Ask your Divine Guardians for protection. Allow the protective waters to soak into every layer of your being. Give thanks to your Allies including the Plant Spirits.

Sacred Herbs

Smudging is the practice of burning herbs, incense or resins for purification and consecration of body, soul and space. Herbal smudges are a wonderful way to cleanse and release energy from your physical space as well as your astral body. Ideal herbs for clearing energy in a smudge are Sage and Cedar. Burn the herbs in a handheld fire-safe vessel as you use your other hand to waft the smoke with a feather, into every corner of your space. When you smudge your astral body, focus on thoroughly saturating each chakra with smoke, starting at the base and moving up from there. My preferred method is to turn counter-clockwise, symbolizing undoing and so that the front, back and sides of my body are all bathed in smoke. I like to smudge the bottoms of my feet and backs of my knees as well. When I smudge space to release energy I move in a counter-clockwise direction towards an open window or door. I move in a clockwise direction when blessing space.

A smudge can be part of a larger ritual or a simple rite of purification all its own. Herbs are not only used for cleansing and releasing, but also for creating the circle, protection, inviting positivity, manifesting power, aiding in grieving, healing and more. For example, sweetgrass is used to invite blessings, mugwort is used for protection and rosemary is used for purification. Herbs can also be used to purify, bless and protect in other ways, besides burning them. For example dried roses can be crushed and sprinkled around the edges of the home as a blessing. Or one could add an infusion of nettle and thyme to her floor cleaning solution to permeate the whole house with psychic protection. The possibilities are endless and we'll explore more in the chapter on plant consciousness.

Dressing the Priestess

You fully step into your Priestess Consciousness when you don the proverbial robe. Maybe it's a special gown and a sacred headdress. Maybe it's a ceremonial necklace, an ancestral amulet, or a pair of magic slippers. Or, if you like to accessorize, perhaps it's all of the above. Whatever your ceremonial dress is, it's yours and it is very special to you. It is comfortable and beautiful and you look forward to putting it on. When you reach the point of stepping into your priestess attire, you are already well inside the labyrinth. You are now prepared to move into the accelerating flow of ritual magic. It is time to step inside the innermost circle, time to sing the song and dance the dance.

Holding Space

A sacred circle can be formed by the bodies of devotees. One might invoke a circle by calling the four quarters or marking the edges of her space with salt. A sacred circle can be permanent or ephemeral in construction.

It can be material, as in made of seashell and stone or simply visualized and traced with a finger. You can pull down a pillar of heavenly light in which to do sacred works. You also can delineate sacred space with sensory or vibratory cues such as burning sacred herbs, ringing bells, blowing horns, chanting or beating drums. This circle is a boundary and a magical amplifier. The sacred circle generates power and light within, while keeping unwelcome energy out.

The most important thing you can do prior to entering into the more vulnerable states of ritual consciousness is to cast the circle. When you enter into mystical realms you require protection and guidance. When you perform your Divine rites you open your most sensitive centers and expand out into your magical space. The circle supports you and contains you, so you are free to open and flow. Whichever kind of circle you choose, speak directly to your Divine Guardians, asking for guidance and protection. Be clear that only Spirit Divine is welcome in your sacred space.

Whether we cast a circle around our ritual space, simply invoke the Light, or enter into a labyrinth, a Medicine Wheel or a drum and dance circle, we extend the idea of a Sacred Center out into the world. By extending this Divinity from within, we expand our light outwards to create a space of love, inviolate. In many contexts and cultures people build Sacred Circles wherein they are safe to pray, worship, give thanks, meditate, commune, perform devotional rituals, receive energy and guidance, create, celebrate, walk ceremonial pathways, dance and heal. As you develop your ways of creating sacred space, consider the multifaceted history of circular altars. Allow different traditions to inform your creative circular processes. Cast your circle and occupy it. You are a Priestess within your circle, upon the earth, spinning and dancing though space.

Pillar of Light

You can invoke the pillar of light anytime at all for protection and uplifting. It is not just reserved for ritual space. In fact, if you'd like to be in the light at all times this is a wonderful way to keep yourself consciously connected to Divine Love and Light on a daily basis. As you go about your day, the pillar moves with you at its center. If you want, you can extend the pillar outwards to include your whole block or your whole town.

Close your eyes and take a few deep breaths. Place your hands in prayer and ask your Guardian Angels for a pillar of light. Pull the heavenly light down and anchor it in the earth with intention and gratitude. Ask for guidance and protection. Visualize the pillar connecting heaven and earth, it spinning all around you, vibrating radiant Divine Light. Make it as big or small as you wish it to be, using the power of your vision.

Circular Altar Building

As you develop your own altar building rituals, you will have your own personal reasons for all the little steps you take to create and enter sacred space. Depending where you are and what kind of magic you are performing you will choose different materials and make different size circles. When I build a circular altar out of sacred objects and offerings, I build my main altar in the north. I mark the remaining directions with smaller altars. I use a compass to ensure that my circle is lined up correctly for the forces of protection to enter. In this way the compass becomes a sacramental talisman, as well as reinforcing my earth consciousness by orienting my body upon the physical earth. I stand in the center of my circle and cast the perimeter with my finger, a wand or a dagger. I focus my mind's eye to create the circle. The edge may be fortified with psychically protective salt or an herbal infusion which I've made. I call on my Angels, Guardians and Guides to enter and hold the space in love and light. I call in Goddess and God. I call in the nature spirits and give thanks to the spirits of the land. I

51

invite the Divine Elemental Spirits of the four directions to enter my circle. I bow in gratitude to the energy of each direction. I personally assign the North as the energy of the earth, the grounding and rooting principle, related to blood, family, foundations and identity. I invite the energy of the East as being the winds of change, the Air element, the source of new beginnings in the turning of the Wheel. The South holds the Fire element, creativity, passion, love. I welcome the special cleansing and healing energy of the West as embodied in the Water element. I also assign animal teachers to each direction, according to spiritual guidance. These elements and animals are represented by objects in the four altars. I proceed with my ritual, meditation, journey, or healing as planned and then close and release the circle in gratitude for any and all wisdom, inspiration, love, blessings and protection that were received.

Grounding and Integration

Grounding describes a feeling of being rooted, in the body, on earth, in life, family and home. It is a sense of being centered, comfortable, present. I believe that it's important to make sure you feel grounded both before and after ritual. A lot of the practices in this chapter are inherently grounding because they celebrate the physicality of the body and the world. Bathing and dressing the body, preparing the ritual space, gathering the forces within the body and cauldron, these things all are centering and homing. Ritual practice can take us out of the material plane to other dimensions, which is wonderful and transformative. When we come back though, the free nature of spirit can sometimes resist coming fully back into its seat within the body, which is why we need to be grounded once again. A feeling of flightiness or very high vibration to the point of physical shaking; feeling light-headed, out of it, floaty; these are signs that your spirit needs to be grounded.

Many rituals end with a grounding ceremony, wherein celebrants gather and eat food together and rehydrate, gently helping each other come back to the ways of the world. Being wrapped tightly in a blanket is grounding. Taking a warm herbal bath will help you integrate your experience. Healing hands upon your feet can ground you. Lying on the ground with your feet in the dirt is very grounding. Hugging a tree is grounding. All things that tell your spirit it is okay to be here in this body, this beautiful world is home for now, it is safe and comfortable here and now; these are grounding phenomena. Ritual can be profoundly detoxifying and thus dehydrating, so rehydration is also essential.

The best way to honor the ritual work you've done is to let it gently and quietly settle into your being. Imagine being at home, having a nice bath with a few drops of Cedarwood essential oil, making some nourishing food, drinking some cool fresh water, wrapping yourself up like a baby and being happy by your hearth fire. Journaling about your experience can help your understanding unfold over the following days. Take your time in identifying and deciphering any messages that may have come through. These are ways of allowing whatever transformations have taken place to fully and safely manifest inside the spiritual channel that is your body.

Chartres

Years ago my grandma and I were visiting Paris and we took the train to Chartres on the one Friday per month that they take all the seats out of the cathedral to reveal the labyrinth set in the floor stones. A soloist was singing in the choir. Pilgrims came from all over the world to walk the labyrinth barefoot and silent, lined up one after the other, twisting and turning back and forth upon the serpentine pathway, slowly journeying to the center of the Goddess Womb, which then delivered each of us back to the world changed from the journey, different, renewed, reborn. This is the power of the ritual. Every step towards the center brings us closer to our most potent truth, our greatest creativity, our deepest peace. Afterwards my grandma and I closed our ritual by sitting in an outdoor café in the shadow of the cathedral, eating delicious mussels in white wine broth with

French fries. As we rode the train back to Paris, I watched Grandma sleep peacefully. Even though we were thousands of miles from home, hurtling through space on a fast train after a long day of pilgrimage, I felt grounded, centered and clear.

Feel Free Ritual

It is my understanding that the word labyrinth has its roots in the word labia, linking the labyrinth symbolically to the unknowable interior of space of the womb. The labyrinth is a maze, a place to lose and find yourself, the primal home of the Minotaur, mirrored in that other place of the creative unconscious, accessed through the labia. This is the gate to and from the magical interior space. Remember that a woman's body is the earth-gate for all humanity. Each of us passed from the world of spirit, through the womb of a mother and out the sacred gate, into this world of form. Woman, you are an earth-gate whether you have birthed children or not. Your dark mysterious spaces are divine and unknowable, yet full of knowing.

With this in mind prepare yourself for a ritual walk in nature. Do a ritual bath of your choice. Dress yourself in a comfortable long skirt or dress with no underpants. If it is cold out, you could wait for a warmer day or just make it a short walk and bundle up with extra layers, but stick with the long skirts and no underwear part. That's important.

Go into nature and leave your gadgets behind. Bring your consciousness to your labia, those outermost gates to the holiest of holies. As you walk pay close attention to what is felt swirling up from the earth below. What information is passed between the outer world and the inner world? What is felt down there? What is known? What is sensed? Perhaps you would like to squat down to get a little closer to the earth, to feel into her emanations. If it is warm out, perhaps you will want to sit on a sun soaked rock, open your legs a bit and allow the breeze to whisper into your moist dark places. If you feel safe and have privacy you might even take a moment to allow a little sun to shine upon the earth gate. As you continue your walk, you might notice how nice it feels to allow unrestricted flowing in this sacred center of your body. You may sense an expansion of a different kind of consciousness. This primal wisdom might feel free and happy. Don't over analyze this. Forget about it and just walk. Lose yourself in the movement of your unfettered body.

Feel free to repeat this ritual whenever the urge arises.

PART II
SACRED VESSEL

CHAPTER SIX

The Temple Guardian

Speak this truth aloud Fierce One: "I am the Temple Guardian. I am custodian of this sacred container of most divine spirit. This vessel is a beautiful gift, worthy of healing and feeling, worthy of preservation and protection. I embody this physical form fully and courageously, with pleasure."

Panther Consciousness: Embodiment

The Temple Guardian is never far from where the Goddess treads. This Priestess Consciousness is symbolized as a cat- a lion, a panther, a tiger, a sphinx cat, or a house cat perhaps. This cat represents self-satisfaction, self-respect and self-esteem. The cat is a fierce protector and symbolizes a deep sensuality and physical embodiment. She reminds us to be fully embodied ourselves, to come all the way down and into the vessel, with pleasure and immense self-worth. The cat is pure instinct and total physical presence. Be fully in your beloved vessel, Lioness. Bring pride and gentle vigilance to guarding the sacred temple that is your physical form.

Get physical in a sensual way. Bring consciousness into every inch of your physical being. Choose some home décor, clothing or jewelry that

59

will help you remember the fierce, passionate, sensuous woman you are. This could come in the image of Goddess, Sekhmet-Bast, a lion, a leopard, a Sphynx Cat, a housecat- whichever feline form most resonates with you. Place these objects and adornments in your space and on your body so that you will be reminded to tap into your Panther Consciousness every day. Perhaps you would benefit from adopting an actual housecat. Bring the teacher into your domain.

The Temple Guardian is also a healer. When she is hurt, she retreats into her lair and licks her wounds. She teaches us that just as we must savor the sweetness in life, when something hurts we must give it expression. The feelings must be fully felt, tasted and known within the body. We must feel through everything, including trauma, grief and loss. Feel the feeling. Know it. Breathe in to it. Allow the pain to express itself. This is how we begin to let go, to forgive, to dissolve emotional blocks and heal the body and soul. Only experience of the feeling within the self leads to its transmutation. Your conscious attention and expression are what heal and transform the wound.

Down and In

The way into the spiritual body is through the physical body. There are many things we can do to be more alive in the physical vessel and really tap into an abundant gratitude for its miraculous nature. It is important to actively work on prioritizing this form of consciousness. We must choose not to become estranged from our physical bodies, our pleasure and pain. Rather, we must fully own and occupy the vessel and all contained therein.

Many practices in this book are designed to heal and bring your spirit home to sit upon the throne within the temple that is your physical form. It may take a lot of work to be at ease occupying your feeling body intimately. If for any reason your ability to trust your instincts and intuition has been damaged or broken, commit to healing this wound first and foremost. Reconnecting to the inner source and wholeheartedly committing to always listening to it is part of the healing process. As you do so, this guidance will become clearer, louder and more constant.

Whether through personal or cultural trauma, it is common in our culture for women to experience a disconnection from their lower chakras. This lower chakra situation needs extra healing for many of us. For some of us, dropping into those lower chakras can stir up some difficult feelings (panic, fight or flight, flashbacks, self-destructive impulses, rage, grief), which can understandably lead to the desire to skip the lower chakra work and just work with the upper chakras- heart opening, eye opening, spirit journeying. However you really do need a strong and vital foundation in the lower realms to safely and effectively explore the worlds of heart and spirit. A tree cannot dance in the sky without a proper root system and a strong trunk to hold it all together. You need those same things too.

Be present to process the emotions that arise from going down into the memories of your personal and cultural wounds. In self-love and self-awareness, know when you are ready to drop in, how deep you are prepared to go and exactly how you are going to take care of yourself afterwards. Have a safe space, a plan and support network to anchor and hold you in your healing. As you feel your healing powers ebb and flow, allow that self-knowledge to determine how and when you take on this work. If your inclination is to go up and out of the body, then work on developing patterns and ways of being that allow you to comfortably move down and into the body, into Panther Consciousness. This is where the wounds are and this is where healing can happen.

If you are in need of healing, you might also consider learning a healing modality such as Reiki. This will give you lifelong skills to deeply care for yourself and loved ones, and will also connect you to a community that you can share healing gifts with.

Carnelian Courage

Carnelian is a crystal which enhances self-trust and can provide the courage and clarity you may need to give voice to your Inner Knower. It helps with navigating boundaries and healing trauma. Carnelian increases one's sense of agency and will to action. Choose a piece of mixed color carnelian to balance the first and second chakras, bringing stability and inspiration within. Carnelian helps us to connect with our earth consciousness, creativity and fertility in all ways. This crystal can rekindle our passions and encourages us to connect into the community we need. You can choose a small piece to carry in your pocket, a piece for under your bed or to place in your work space. Use carnelian in your ritual circles and meditations.

Body Mind Awareness Meditation

Stand with your feet hip's width apart, knees soft and unlocked, tailbone slightly curled forward. Let your strong abdominal core lift the rib cage up to allow the lungs to fill and the solar plexus to expand into space. With vertebrae perfectly stacked, roll your shoulders up and back, letting the arms hang loose at your sides. Imagine a string in the center of your crown pulling your skeleton up into gentle alignment. Breathe into the body. Bring your awareness to your feet connecting energetically to the earth. Feel the stabilizing force of gravity.

Feel your life force rising up through your legs from the ground. Let each inhale bring your awareness up, scanning each chakra, each joint, each organ, each muscle for data. Scan the front of your body and then the back. On each exhale allow your chin to gently bow forward, stretching the back of the neck and the shoulders. On each inhale let the chin rise slightly while keeping the neck long.

As you explore this posture and gentle breath for a few minutes, just observe. Let the feelings and sensations rise into your consciousness. How does it feel in your body? When you focus on deepening your breath do you start to feel immediate surrender to the rhythm? Is there a struggle? Do you want to run away? Or can you let it be easy? Do you love being in that fabulous vessel of yours? Do you love to fill up your lungs with energy and feel it moving freely through your being? Do you love to animate the flesh of you? When something hurts do you send love and light to it to dissolve the pain? Or do you put a wall around it like the oyster makes a pearl around a grain of sand?

If there are any areas of pain or resistance, experiment with sending breath into them. Notice how deep you can go by staying present to the discomfort while releasing it through the exhale. Notice if your intention, breath and focus are actually dissolving those areas of tension. Pay attention to any wisdom or healing energy flowing through the body. And if there are unpleasant emotions, just keep breathing as you allow the emotions to move through you. If there are tears, let them flow out.

Soul of the Warrior: She who is Fierce

There is a warrior within you. She is an aspect of the Temple Guardian. She is fierce and fearless. Her instincts are sharp as knives and she knows how to fight. Righteous and primal, she awakens to protect, when real threats appear. Her will is Divine. Her territory is vast. She is patient, enduring and dutiful. Her vigil is constant, her mission singular and her spirit indomitable.

As you traverse the territories of your life, it can be comforting just knowing you have this Inner Guardian. There is no need to fear her, nor deny her. She is in you and one day you may need all her primal wisdom, strength and courage. She provides all that is needed. In times of sickness, grief or trauma, it is she who will keep you. Embrace this inner Goddess aspect and pull her from the shadows. You can activate this archetype within yourself by fiercely protecting yourself and serving your purpose, your creations and your people. Strive to be true to your path, deep in your faith and indomitable in your spirit- as She is.

If you are not sure you have this Inner Guardian; if you cannot remember ever feeling her fierce consciousness take over your mind and body; if there ever was a time that you felt you failed to protect yourself; then this aspect of self may be in need of healing and cultivation. Alternatively your Inner Guardian could be overly active or hypervigilant as a result of past traumas. Is your Inner Guardian in balance? Does she need expression? Is she repressed or does she need soothing? Perhaps she needs cultivation and expression through an activity which enhances your instincts, confidence and protective qualities, such as: community/ environmental/ political activism, animal rescue, falconry, marksmanship, fencing, archery, martial arts, yoga, dance, primal screaming, walking and hiking outdoors.

When you are confident in your ability to protect your physical body and express the fierceness within your soul, then the Inner Guardian can rest until she is truly needed. When you are able to take care of yourself in this way, then this warrior power surges in abundance, which you can then extend to defend your loved ones, your community and the earth itself.

Grace: Let it be Easy

While we benefit from developing our inner warrior spirit, there is no need to see life as a battle. In fact you can simply let it be easy, when you know you are supported by the Inner Guardian. When you completely align with your purpose and your path, even the greatest feats can take on effortlessness. In gaining experience in your skills, by being single-minded in your devotion, all your effort flows in a unified force. When you are singular, dedicated, the best you can be, it can be easy- win or lose. You simply do your best as you flow towards mastery. When you know you are serving your purpose, there is no need to struggle. You are right where you are meant to be.

You are tested, you are forged in fire, but with Faith, you trust that the winding way leads to Fruition. Even failures are filled with rich teachings, to be assimilated and transformed through your Alchemical processes. Every defeat is coded with information that ultimately will lead to an important victory of the spirit. Flowing through the trials and tribulations with this easy perspective will get you where you need to go. It is the Grace which matters most. Never lose faith. Know that you are not alone. May the road rise up to meet you and if instead a flood comes down the mountain and washes the road away, do not despair. Open your heart, surrender and ask Goddess and God to show you the way. If you are weak ask for strength. If you are shattered, cry out to be made whole again. Trust that one day these lessons will serve a greater purpose. Your faith allows you to accept challenges as an essential part of becoming the woman you are meant to be.

Being secure in your powers, you can go through life as gentle as can be. Being centered deep within, you bring forth with grace, you traverse with ease and focus. Aligned and in harmony, you create your world and you dance your path- even when you must dance with your sword and your shield. In self-awareness you identify the ways you need to change, but you use a kind and loving hand and a blessed magical dagger to cut away that which no longer serves, to transform what remains. In your connected-consciousness you accept the ebb and flow of life. To struggle is unnecessary. You do your best, you focus and you succeed or you fail. So be it.

Pray for Grace

"Goddess: Please let me flow with purpose and grace. Please show me the path of ease and alignment."

Panther Practice

I now ask you to make a willing sacrifice of your own perceived limitations for the sake of your personal and spiritual growth. Choose a new physical practice that meets the following criteria: something you've never done before and are not inherently good at; something challenging that both scares you and excites you; something that enhances your Panther Consciousness. Go outside your comfort zone. If you think you have no rhythm, take a West African dance class. If you don't believe in your Inner Warrior, learn Kung Fu. If you have a hard time staying present in your body, try Kundalini Yoga. If you have trouble accessing your sacred sensual nature, try belly dancing. Take a couple of days to think about what is right for you and then go for it! Do the research and find out what local opportunities are available to you and then go out for the team, apply, sign up or show up! Let your warrior spirit carry you through any awkward phases of your growth and learning process. Trust in the fire which forges you.

CHAPTER SEVEN
Plant Consciousness

There are so many ways that plants give to us, so very many doors they open for us. Plants are healers, teachers and wisdom keepers. Plants are magical enchanters. Plants are beautiful dancers. Plants are generous friends. Plants are funny. Plants are great company. Plants love to be loved. Plants have a wonderful balance between doing and being, reminding us to perhaps do less and be more. Look at all the green patterns they make. Let those patterns into your soul. Let those plant patterns soothe your eyes and reweave your consciousness in remembrance of the sacred relationship between you and all of nature. Those patterns are a part of the same tapestry into which you are woven. You are a mystical creature in a most divine garden.

Enter the Divine Garden

The flowering tree within you is a direct expression of your divine nature, a spiritual structure within your subtle body. As we were created in the Garden, we inherited many systems of plantlike structure- the glandular systems, the nervous system and the circulatory system for example. Behold your spiritual tree, as reflected through your physical and emotional health, around which the serpents of your energetic life force coil and climb.

By embracing and fostering consciousness within this subtle, sensitive system, you can uncover a layer of magical existence within your very own plant body. As you become closer to the Great Mother, the Green One, she unlocks the mysteries of the Tree of Life within you. Her embrace fills you with health, healing power, wisdom, knowledge and Divinity. By tapping into plant consciousness you send your roots deep within the earth, receiving the grounding forces of the underworld, the iron core, the chthonic realm.

Communing directly with the plant world can accelerate your spiritual journey infinitely, by refining the subtle body within the body of form. Let the plants speak to you. Allow yourself to see the plants and hear which ones might be whispering to you. By eating your greens and drinking your teas, by tasting the fruit, by ingesting or burning sacred herbs, by planting your garden and walking in the forest, by hugging a tree you enter communion with nature. Through plant communion you become connected to the natural world without and also to that most secret inner garden within, as the vastness of your consciousness expands into increasingly more peaceful, grounded and perceptive pathways.

Plant Pattern Meditation

There is a plant pattern that is calling to you now. Maybe you already know what it is as you read these words. If not, take a few days or hours to generally tune into and observe plant patterns: moss in the woods, trees dancing in the sky in your backyard, tall grasses at the botanical garden, a field of flowering corn. Some particular plant pattern is calling to you. When you know what it is, go find it and sit with it.

Bring a blanket or whatever you need to sit and be comfortable for at least twenty minutes. Allow the plant pattern into your soul through your eyes. Let it touch, heal and soothe you. Breathe and let the plant patterns be your only thought. Send love to the plant spirits. Send appreciation.

Receive the gift of their pattern in your heart. Receive the gift of their personality, their grace, their essence. At the end of your meditation ask if the plant spirits have a message. Close your eyes and wait for any images, ideas, feelings, words or other clues that may come through. Close your meditation with an offering (of water or corn meal perhaps) and a bow of gratitude. When you get home journal about your experience.

Plants have shown me that the number of beautiful patterns to focus on is infinite. If I find myself heading into a negative thought loop I simply remind myself of the wisdom, peace, mystery and beauty of the plants all around me. The plants are real and they are here now. For me the pattern of leaves dancing in the breeze against the sky is so powerfully soothing that it can immediately replace any other thought pattern I don't want to spend my time with. That gorgeous green pattern brings great peace and freedom to my heart. There is so much healing and soothing that nature provides. The pattern you focus on can be whatever you want it to be. Your focus is your power. Your pattern is your choice.

The Yellow Rose

In April of 2014 I bought a bouquet of cut flowers from the grocery store. There were a few roses in the bouquet, which lasted longer than the other flowers. One of the roses miraculously began making a bunch of tiny new green leaves and shoots so I trimmed the stem and placed it in water in a clear glass vase to see if it would also begin to send out roots. Sure enough it made lots of roots, so then I planted it in an old take-out rice carton to see if it would become a rose bush. In June I took a trip to Los Angeles and saw my Spiritual Teacher Nicole. In that session my Guides made it clear that I could quit my day job whenever I felt ready and begin my new venture full time.

I thought about my rose on the trip, wondering if it would still be alive when I got back to Brooklyn. It was. It outgrew the rice carton and was transplanted to a ten gallon pot where it thrived. It filled out the pot and even made two rosebuds. The flowers were small and bright yellow. Two weeks after I got home to Brooklyn my husband received an unexpected raise and promotion, making it suddenly possible for me to quit my day job. The yellow rose delivered the message of a promising new beginning. This promise came into my life in the spring and revealed itself in the summer with the blossoming of the yellow buds. The miraculous rose which I cared for and cultivated taught me to treat my new projects with the same reverence and awe. The rose helped me believe that my new endeavors would reach the same expression of fruition as the delicate flowers. These are the gentle signs of encouragement my Guides will give me, so long as I am willing to open my eyes, to believe and to reach into my own blossoming.

Buds with Buds

Consider saying something nice to a living plant today. Just wait until no one is looking, find yourself a nice plant buddy to appreciate and then just reach out your hands and say something along the lines of, "Wow, you are amazing! Thank you!" You might feel some embarrassment or resistance to this idea. But if you can get past that, just let yourself really appreciate the plant's beautiful spirit with your open heart. Be with the energy of the plant. Let it come to you. And if it's a big strong tree, feel free to give it a hug.

Poison Ivy

My mom is a hippie. When she was pregnant with my older brother she lived in a cabin with no door in the town of Montague, MA. There was a wood stove and an old armchair that had an active bumble-bee nest in it. It had no running water or any sort of plumbing. There was a tree growing through it and it was in the middle of a field of poison ivy. The previous spring when the poison ivy leaves were just appearing my mom began eating them, one leaf per day, to develop immunity to poison ivy, according to a book she had on Indigenous Medicine.

After that she never again got a rash from poison ivy and neither have my brother or I in our entire lives and we have been exposed to it quite regularly. The town of Montague had my mom evicted from her cabin, offended at the idea of a pregnant woman living in a shack with no running water through the winter. She and my dad moved to a commune in Bolton, MA where she gave birth. My mom likes to say that my brother Sam was conceived under a tree and born on a hippie commune. This story of origin pleases her to no end.

Honoring Plant Spirits

When it comes to working with plant medicines it is of great importance to honor the spirit of the herb. Let it be a priority for you to connect with the spirit of each plant and express appreciation, whether you harvested it yourself or received it in the mail. The best way to do that is through true reverence for a plant's essence, and simple offerings of gratitude.

Sing, talk and make offerings to your beloved plants. Connect into the whole garden and embrace your earthy wisdom. Develop loving relationships with healing plants. Each plant has its own story to share. Plants have spirit, consciousness, memory, emotion, profound intelligence and great sensitivity. They are expressions of the Divine, every bit as much as we are. By embracing this truth, a world of wholeness, connection, wonder and healing opens to us. The Green One has left many secrets in safekeeping with the plants. When you are ready, the plants will gladly share their wisdom.

When harvesting, open a channel of communication. My mom taught me to hold the plant in hand gently, saying "May I?" to the Plant Spirit, before cutting with a sharp blade. Treat the plant spirit with respect and gratitude. Create a pathway of empathy. You can usually feel that the plant is generous and willing to give of itself. And if you don't feel that, then maybe the plant is telling you something. What is the plant trying to tell you? Sometimes the insects and worms will tell you things too. You are their ally. You all live in the same garden and want the best life for one another.

The Corn Maiden

Liv Wheeler, the Kontomble Diviner I met under the Grandmother Redwood, is a frequent guest on the wonderful and amazing "Dream Freedom Beauty" podcast. On a recent episode the Little People asked that any listeners living on American soil, but not of native descent, make offerings of corn meal to the Corn Maiden as an expression of gratitude for her immense generosity and hospitality. This, like most of the messages Liv translates from the Little People, resonated with me and I went ahead and made some offerings of corn meal.

At that time we were just coming into corn harvest season in my part of the world and so I picked up the first ears of fresh corn I saw at the local market and brought them home to my mom's for a full moon ritual. We performed a little ceremony in her garden and left an ear of corn for the Corn Maiden in a bowl with some other seasonal offerings.

A week later I was visiting my mom again and we saw that the corn was still there, undisturbed by any of the many local critters, and every single kernel on one side had sprouted new corn seedlings. Neither of us had ever seen corn do this before and my mom being an avid gardener who has experience growing corn called it a miracle. I took it as a sign that the Corn Maiden was pleased with our offering.

The next week I was on vacation in corn country and we were eating fresh picked local corn every day. There always seemed to be an extra ear or two left over and I would take them along with other snacks out to an altar in the woods and make offerings. There were animal families with babies on the land including deer, bunnies, raccoons, groundhogs, foxes and coyotes. The animals ate those offerings every night.

On the night of the new moon, while I was there on the land I performed a ceremony where I entered into the visionary realm. I found myself in a radiant glowing temple made of corn kernels. White, yellow, orange, blue and purple kernels formed the temple dome around the base of which there were tiles with vertical ears of corn on them with the husk still on and peeled back at the top with a little bit of the corn and corn silk showing.

The Corn Maiden showed herself to me as a native woman with long flowing black hair standing in the middle of a corn field. Then she showed herself to me as the corn itself. She made it clear that every single corn kernel is her sacred Goddess flesh and that her only desire is to feed the people, the animals, and then in cycling back to the earth, to feed the plants with her sacred body.

I felt that she revealed herself to me partly because I showed her gratitude and love but also because I had helped her to feed the beloved animals. It being the height of her growing season, her essence was able to come through with crystal clarity. I was stunned to receive this gift from the Corn Maiden, and overwhelmed at the magnitude of her beauty, her sweetness, her gentleness, her selflessness, her singular and indiscriminate desire to feed and grow all living things. I am so humbled and grateful to have communed with this Goddess, perhaps the greatest nurturer the earth has ever known. The revelations she showed me opened an endless source of wonder and love towards abundant nature and set an example for me as to how to give forth and nourish the life around me.

I pass this request on to you from the Little People – please make an offering of sacred corn to the Corn Maiden in gratitude for her boundless generosity and hospitality. May you receive her nurturing, body and soul.

May you return that nourishment to the Goddess and all the beloved children of earth.

Plant Allies

There are many ways we can reciprocate all that plants do for us. They feed us. They heal us. They clothe us. They clean our air. They clean and nourish our soil. They fill our world with beauty. They balance, open and stimulate our senses and our spirits. By planting native non-GMO seeds we help the plant world. By eating non-GMO organic foods we strongly support a healthy ecosystem. By eating locally produced foods, especially from our own gardens, we contribute to the healing of the earth.

Another way we can ally with the plants is by allying with their allies: pollinators. The ubiquitous use of pesticides, environmental pollution, loss of habitat and even light pollution are all threatening important species of pollinators. At this moment in time many pollinators need our help.

Planting a pollinator garden is one simple thing we can do to support the pollinators and the plants. By planting native seeds favored by pollinators we are helping to restore balance to our ecosystem. Even if you live in the city you can still help the pollinators by throwing some pollinator seed bombs into an abandoned lot, alongside a bike path or down by the river. Find a crack in the pavement and sprinkle in some milkweed seeds and see what happens. In the summer you might just get some monarch butterflies fluttering down for some much needed nourishment.

Native hardy plants can do a lot with a little, as can our pollinator friends. These small gestures can feel empowering in a big way and will serve to activate the plant ally inside of you. Become a warrior for the butterflies and the bees. Fight for the moths and the hummingbirds, armed with flowers, seeds and your great love of nature.

Herbal Apothecary

When you feel called to explore the world of healing herbs, begin by choosing a small selection of herbs to work with and become familiar. This will allow you to be undaunted by the vast amounts of herbal knowledge out there and to focus on a few herbs that speak to you in the present. The Herbal Compendium below covers a variety of herbs which you may like to include in your herbal cabinet. Healing and Magical attributes will be explored. These herbs are powerful and when used correctly can change one's life, restoring both health and spirit. Some are consumed as vegetables and cooking herbs. Others are taken as infusions or decoctions. Roots, stems, leaves, flowers and fruits impart herbal healing. The absolute best way to learn herbal wisdom is through healing your own body, mind and soul with careful communion, one herb at a time.

Herbal Classifications

Alterative- an agent capable of altering an unhealthy body, restoring normal bodily function over time

Anodyne- pain reliever

Anthelmintic- acts against parasitic infections

Astringent- constricts tissue, restricting flow of bodily fluid

Carminative- gas relief

Demulcent- soothes mucous membrane

Diaphoretic- increases sweating

Diuretic- increases urine

Emetic- causes vomiting

Emmenagogue- agent that stimulates menstrual flow (not for pregnant women)

Febrifuge- fever reducer

Hypotensive- lowers blood pressure

Nervine- soothes nervous excitement

Vulnerary- wound healer

Tips and Precautions

Dried leaf and flower herbs are mostly **"infused"** which means boiled water is poured over them and then allowed to sit for 20-30 minutes, gently releasing the essence into the infusion, before straining. Depending upon the density or lightness of these herbs and their taste you would use between a teaspoon and a ¼ cup herbs per one cup of water. You can generally adjust the ratio of herbs to water according to your personal taste.

Dried roots are most often **"decocted"** which is to say: gently simmered on a stovetop for twenty minutes before straining. An alternative to this method is to do an overnight infusion- the extended time allows the woody roots to open up and release more of the medicine. While you do need to plan ahead, you won't need to spend time watching the stovetop. Yet another alternative is to do a half and half technique- Decoct for ten minutes and then allow to infuse for a few hours before straining. Chopped roots usually take between a tsp and a tbsp. per cup of water depending on taste.

Make a **poultice** of dried herbs (heaped in the bottom of a bowl), by pouring just enough boiled water over the top of the herbs. It should not be soupy, but barely wet. Use a fork to press the dry leaves down into the damp mash. Cover the bowl to let the leaves steam open for a few minutes and allow to cool. Apply the poultice either directly to the skin or in a cheesecloth bandage for a half hour or so. If you have fresh picked leaves or flowers simply drop them into boiled water for twenty seconds which should be enough to open them up/ release the medicine, and allow to cool before applying as a poultice.

Herbal vinegars are made by pouring cider vinegar (you can use room temperature vinegar or heat the vinegar to a brief simmer to help open up the herbs) over fresh herbs and letting them steep for a couple of weeks in a jar with a lid. Agitate the infusion once a day. Herbal vinegars can be enjoyed for months.

When working with a **new herb**, use that herb individually at first, so that you can be clear exactly which effects are associated with that particular herb. Once you feel well acquainted with specific herbs you may desire to mix herbal blends to achieve more layered healing solutions.

If you have the opportunity to **wild forage herbs**, be sure not to harvest from potentially toxic earth or polluted air (industrial sites/ pesticides/ road side). Never take more than your fair share; leave plenty for other foragers, for the birds and bees, as well as for the plant itself to regenerate. If you do plan to wild forage make sure not to forage endangered species.

If you plan to dry your **herbal harvest** rather than using the herbs fresh, pick the herbs in late morning on a sunny day after the dew has dried. Hang them upside down in bundles or spread them on drying screen. Wait until they are completely dried out (so they don't mold) before storing them in jars in a cool, dry, dark cupboard. Roots can take months to dry. Place them in a paper bag. When they break with a snap they are dry and can be stored in a jar or tin.

If you have a garden, plant herbs from seed or transplant them from a friend's garden. There is great joy in waiting and watching as your seed babies sprout and grow.

Alteratives are highly effective when taken consistently for an extended period. For example you might drink one pot of Dandelion root tea per day, four or five out of seven days a week, for three or four months on end.

Emmenagogues are taken just prior to, and during the first day or two of menstruation. They are best not taken internally at any other point in the moon cycle and never by pregnant women. They shouldn't be taken internally by those with an overly heavy menstrual flow or those with a short cycle (less than 28 days). In our compendium, if an herb is an emmenagogue, this will be the first property listed as it should be the first property considered in whether or not this is the right herb for you at the moment. Emmenagogues can really impact your menstrual cycle/flow and should be used accordingly.

These are the herbs I love and the preparations I use most. Maybe the perfect herb for your body will be found in another book, or may even call out to you as you walk in the field. If you find herbal healing interesting, there is so much to learn and so many fun directions you can go in; such as making your own salves, essences and tinctures or brewing Dandelion Wine.

Everyday Tea Recipes

CLEAR SKIN TEA

Make an overnight infusion of 2 Tbsp Burdock root, 1 tsp Elder Flower, 1 tsp Chrysanthemum in a 4 cup teapot

DIVINATION TEA

Decoct 4 Tbsp Dandelion root in 4 cups water

CALM NERVES TEA

Make an infusion of 2 Tbsp Rooibos, 1 Tbsp chopped Reishi, 2 tsp
Oatstraw in a 4 cup teapot

WOMEN'S EVERY DAY HEALTH TEA

Infuse, 2 Tbsp Raspberry leaf, 1 Tbsp Nettle, and 1 tsp Oatstraw in a 4
cup teapot

Herbal Compendium

Astragalus- Anti-inflammatory. Antioxidant. Immune booster. Liver and
spleen support. Adrenal tonic. Treats stress, thyroid imbalance, chronic
fatigue, allergies, stomach ulcers. Beneficial to those with diabetes and
auto-immune disease. Decoct the roots or add to homemade broths and
soups for the last 20 minutes of cooking.

Burdock Root- Alterative. Antibacterial. Antifungal. Anti-inflammatory.
Antioxidant. Anti-diabetic (high in inulin, a blood sugar stabilizer).
Diaphoretic. Diuretic. Good for all manner of swelling. Nourishing and
tonifying for skin, kidney, liver and mucous membranes. Treats gout,
jaundice, asthma, eczema and acne. Excellent bath herb. Fresh roots are
available in Asian markets for cooking (Gobo). As well as eating the fresh
roots as vegetables, the dried roots can be decocted. Associated with the
Goddess Venus. Makes a protective amulet.

Celery Root, Stalk, Leaf and Seed- Emmenagogue (the seed). Antifungal.
Anti-inflammatory. Antioxidant. Hypotensive. Carminative. Good for
liver and spleen. Nervine tonic. Mild diuretic. Urinary antiseptic. Treats
gout and kidney stones by removing uric acid. Alkaline. Vitamins A, C,
Potassium, Folate. This whole vegetable (root, stalk, leaf and seed) can be
eaten and used in all manner of culinary applications. Magically used for
psychic development, divination, beauty and love.

Chrysanthemum/ Ju hua cha- Antioxidant. Anti-inflammatory. Stimulates digestion (In China the tea is frequently served with a greasy meal). Soothes skin and strengthens eyes. Nervine properties. Calms the liver. Treats cold and flu symptoms such as headache and congestion. Improves lung and cardiovascular health. Prepare as an infusion. Excellent bath herb. Magically used for protection.

Comfrey Root and Leaf- Cellular proliferant: promotes quick healing of skin and bone. Emollient. Mucilaginous. Apply topical poultice to fungal infections, bruises, sprains and breaks. Relieves inflammation of the eye. Never use comfrey on wounds where there is a possibility of infection (animal bites, puncture wounds etc.) as comfrey's cellular proliferation activity will very likely heal the outer skin and seal in the infection. If you are certain that there is no risk of underlying infection, comfrey can be used topically to heal damaged skin such as scrapes, minor burns and scars. Comfrey is usually best used externally due to the fact that it is not good for the liver. Situations in which you might consider careful administration of comfrey internally, would be to heal broken bones or to treat stomach ulcers. In such cases comfrey should be used sparingly and only by individuals with healthy livers. Prepare as a poultice or as an infusion. An excellent bath herb. Associated with Goddess Hecate. Used in ritual cleansing.

Dandelion- Alterative. Anti-inflammatory. Antioxidant. Diaphoretic. Diuretic. Blood sugar stabilizer. Good for all manner of swelling. Nourishing and tonifying for skin, spleen, liver and gall bladder. Digestive aid. Treats PMS and menstrual bloat. Regulates hormones. Treats eczema and acne. Brightens eyes. Available as a leafy vegetable at most health food stores. Greens can be eaten raw in salad or cooked. The dried leaves make an infusion. The roots are decocted or infused overnight. The flowers are used for making Dandelion Wine and Dandelion Jelly. Associated with Goddess Hecate. Enhances psychic ability. Used for divination.

Elder Flower- Alterative. Immune booster. Febrifuge. Antiseptic. Anti-inflammatory. Diaphoretic. Diuretic. Expectorant. Use for congestion and all manner of respiratory complaints. Cures influenza. Astringent. Treats inflammation of the skin, eyes and throat. Treats edema and improves kidney function. An infusion is made of the flowers. **If you harvest your own flowers be very careful to remove all of the tiny stems as the stems are emetic (cause vomiting).** Excellent bath herb. Associated with the fairy realm and Norse Goddess Hel.

Feverfew- Emmenagogue. Anti-inflammatory. Antispasmodic. Febrifuge. Heart tonic. Treats and prevents migraine. Good for headache and earache. Feverfew can be used magically for protection.

Garlic- One raw clove per day will surely keep the doctor away. Immune booster. Antibacterial. Anthelmintic. Detoxifying. Supports heart health. Antiviral. Used for psychic protection and exorcism. Associated with Hecate.

Ginger- Warming. Immune booster. Antiviral. Soothes nausea. Improves digestion. Stabilizes blood sugar. Antioxidant. Magically increases power and energy.

Lavender- Emmenagogue. Carminative. Antibiotic. Antispasmodic. Nervine tonic. Hypotensive. Sleep aid. Mood lifter. Use in sachets, dream pillows and baths. Make an infusion with the flowers. Magically used for love, purification and clarity. Associated with Hecate, the heart chakra and snakes. Celebrate the summer by burning dried lavender.

Lemon Balm/ Melissa- Emmenagogue. Anti-anxiety. Nervine tonic. Uplifting of the mood and emotions. Mild sedative. Uterine tonic. Bee ally. Associated with Jupiter.

Mugwort- Emmenagogue. Antispasmodic. Mild sedative. Anthelmintic. Anesthetic. Antibacterial. Antifungal. Dream enhancer. Herbs from the Artemisia family should never be taken internally for more than one week at a time. Use sparingly for liver stimulant properties. Good for sluggish digestion/ constipation. Nervine properties. The leaves are infused. Excellent bath herb and smudge herb for protection, healing and divination. Use mugwort tea to cleanse your crystals. Associated with Artemis and Hecate.

Oatstraw- Alterative. Demulcent. Nervine tonic. Heart tonic. Lowers cholesterol. Nourishing and restorative. Skin soothing. Strengthens endocrine and nervous systems. Hormone regulator. High in A, B and E vitamins. High in minerals such as calcium, magnesium, iron and zinc. Makes an infusion. Good bath herb. Magically attracts prosperity.

Onion- An onion a day keeps the doctor away. Anti-inflammatory. Antiseptic. Vulnerary. Immune booster. High in vitamins and minerals. Supports heart and eye health. Antifungal. Anthelmintic. Antiviral. Diaphoretic.

Raspberry Leaf- Uterine tonic. Astringent. Strengthens pelvic muscles and uterus. Treats PMS, pregnancy and labor. Regulates hormones. Treats nausea, diarrhea, stomach ache, gas and cramps. Antiseptic. Adrenal tonic. Treats thrush, urinary tract infection, mouth sores. Strengthens gums. Good for bones and teeth. High in Vitamins C and B, magnesium, potassium. Makes an infusion. Magically used for happiness and love.

Red Clover- Alterative. Antibiotic. Anti-inflammatory. Antispasmodic. Antioxidant. Expectorant. Diuretic. Estrogenic. Uterine tonic. Appetite suppressant. Regulates menses. Aids circulation and cardiovascular health. Blood thinner. Good for lungs, liver, skin, kidneys and immune system. Promotes lactation. Treatment for menopause and PMS symptoms. High in calcium, magnesium, potassium, Vitamins C and B. Makes an infusion. Magically used for fidelity in love. Associated with Wadjet (Uto) and faeries.

Reishi- Anti-anxiety. Anti-inflammatory. Immune booster. Antifungal. Anti-histamine. Anti-tumor. Promotes healing and toning of heart, liver, kidney and brain. Add chopped dried Reishi to your broths and teas.

Rooibos/ Red Bush- Antioxidant. Anti-inflammatory. Soothes skin conditions. Nervine tonic. Antispasmodic. Antihistamine. Antiviral. Aids digestion. Relieves gas and constipation. High in vitamin C, iron, potassium, calcium, magnesium, zinc, manganese, fluoride. Can be used to aid in dream work.

Rose Flower- Emmenagogue. Nervine. Astringent. Mood lifter. Antibacterial. Antiseptic. Aphrodisiac. Promotes circulation and nourishes the heart. Eye, skin and hair wash. Anti-inflammatory. Tonic for gall bladder and liver- increases bile production. Balances hormones. Treats menstrual cramps. Drink the tea for prophetic dreams. Place one rose in water upon your altar for luck in love. Grow roses in your garden to attract faeries. Associated with Goddess Venus.

Rosemary- Antioxidant. Vulnerary. Antiseptic. Astringent. Stimulates healing and circulation. Shields brain from free radicals. Tones skin. Treats dandruff. Rosemary is a wonderful cooking herb and can also be used as an infusion. Magically attracts faeries. Burn to purify air and receive knowledge.

Sage- Emmenagogue. Antioxidant. Anti-inflammatory. Insulin booster. Astringent. Carminative. Cools fever and soothes sore throat. Stimulates digestion. Tonic for nervous system. Tones blood, liver and kidneys. **Should not be used by those who have had any form of seizure as Sage has epileptiform convulsant properties.** Can be used to wean babies and is therefore contraindicated for nursing mothers. Use sage in cooking or as an infusion. Sacred herb used to release and purify energy through smudging. Also burnt to attract wisdom and overcome grief.

Stinging Nettle- Alterative. Astringent. Anti-inflammatory. Antioxidant. Anti-spasmodic. Diuretic. Anthelmintic. Decongestant. Febrifuge. Expectorant. Uterine tonic. Safe for pregnancy and nursing (increases lactation). Treats PMS symptoms such as water retention and heavy bleeding. Stabilizes blood sugar. Treats hay fever- natural antihistamine. High in iron, it treats chronic fatigue and anemia. Removes acid and inflammation. Stimulates digestion. Stimulates adrenal glands. Urinary tract tonic. Treats and prevents kidney problems. Restores shine to hair. Treats dandruff. High in vitamins C, A and K. Wear gloves when handling fresh nettles. Once blanched or dried the sting is removed. When fresh spring nettles can be had, eat them as a cooked green vegetable. Dried nettles can be infused. To magically protect your home, sprinkle dried nettle around the edges of your domain. Effective in purification baths.

Sweetgrass- Used primarily as a smudge herb for purification, spiritual cleansing, attracting sweetness, positivity and blessings.

Thyme- Antispasmodic. Antifungal. Expectorant. Anthelmintic. Antiseptic without irritating skin or mucosae. Stimulates circulatory, respiratory and nervous systems. Immune booster- works on thymus gland to stimulate T-cell production. Eat delicious fresh or dried thyme in your cooking or make an infusion. Enhances psychic protection. Burn it or wear it as an amulet.

Turmeric- Anti-inflammatory. Antioxidant. Antimicrobial. Digestive stimulant. Blood thinner. Heart tonic. Fresh turmeric roots can be found in health food stores. Chopped or ground roots are commonly available. Use turmeric in your cooking, broths, teas and vinegars.

CHAPTER EIGHT

Blood

Menstrual blood is the essence, the symbol and the evidence of our divine creative power. The fertile chaos that is the Goddess' womb is exalted most especially in our cleansing and creative blood rhythms. I invite you now to return to the Red Tent. The flaps of this Red Tent are open wide for your homecoming. You are so welcome, wanted and held here in the sacred space of menstruation. Every woman should have the space and time to menstruate properly- a period of quiet celebration where all energy is going towards releasing, clearing, making way for the creative womb to prepare itself once again.

Take a moment to marvel at this clock-like lunar mechanism. Remember how this wisdom has been ticking away inside you since before your first period. There is nothing inconvenient or unclean about it. It is a sacred dance with the moon and the earth. Dance your moon dance with grace and harmony. Being born with a uterus is a gift and a privilege in itself. By remembering how to honor your womb and the power within, much pain and suffering are transcended.

Flow Slow

Menstruation should not be painful. If there is pain then changes should be made. The pain should not be medicated for it is a message from your womb. The underlying cause of the pain is what needs to be addressed. Menstruation is not a disease and should not be treated as such. You do not need pills or products that allow you to control it or pretend it's not happening. You need to take the time to bleed with intention, to go within, to bring your consciousness into your womb as your blood flows, unhindered, outward. When we ignore, disrespect or suppress our natural flowing, this is when the womb rebels and starts acting out. When we invert the beauty of our blessing it starts to feel like a curse.

If you do suffer from difficult periods, see what happens if you stop wearing tampons (for some women this is the only change they need to make). Also consider taking a three month course of alterative herbs. Alteratives are herbs that gently ease the body back into balance, restoring healthy function over an extended treatment period. They are considered blood cleaners, tonic to liver, digestion and elimination systems. Dandelion root tea, for example, is an excellent alterative. Alteratives address longstanding, underlying issues and deficiencies that contribute to hormonal imbalance.

Menstruation is an alchemy all its own and the balance and harmony required to menstruate well is the same. If you are struggling with, suppressing, subverting, ignoring, stifling and stigmatizing your blood in any way, I invite you now to stop. Instead, align with the beautiful, wise, life-giving power of your womb. Simply being present to and experiencing the flow of your sacred life-giving blood is essential. Slow down to anticipate what is required next: rest, yoga, deep breath, nourishing food or a walk in the woods.

Open the channel to your womb; listen to and nurture this part of yourself. See how your body responds to your attention, intention and preparation. Give yourself permission to be in the internal space of menstruation: make this a priority and see how things change when you go with the wisdom of your own flow. Practice a sacred way of menstruating. Begin from the womb and from there ripple your magic out into each successive concentric circle of your life. Go to the center and live from there.

Healing with Dandelion

This is one lesson I learned the hard way and how I healed myself. I share this story because I believe that many women in my culture and generation grew up acting and thinking similarly and I hope it can help someone else empower her own Inner Healer.

I started having menstrual cramps in high school. When it came to menstruation, I aspired to be like the girl in the tampon commercial- you know the one in the white jeans, with the flawless complexion, laughing and having fun in the sun? I wanted to pretend it wasn't happening. I refused to let it stop me from doing my thing.

And that's how it started- my womb-denying way of menstruating. After twenty years of working and socializing right through my periods I was due for a healing crisis. I wore tampons, constrictive clothes, bad shoes. I popped ibuprofen and acetaminophen. The longer I denied the true nature of menstruation the worse my cramps got over the years, especially following a surgery to remove an ovarian cyst. I routinely took sixteen extra strength pain killers to get through the first two days of my period. Then I got sick with a lot of vomiting and could no longer keep those pills down.

I didn't go to a doctor because I knew I simply needed to change my thinking in order to fix my doing and heal my being. I did a four month course of Dandelion Root tea, during which time I went through a full pound of dried dandelion roots. I stopped taking pain pills and wearing tampons completely and started to gradually bring more and more intention to menstruating well.

The vomiting episodes ceased immediately and I have not had one single menstrual cramp in the five years since I made these changes. In the process of being empowered through herbs, knowing my body and practicing self-care, I am remembering how to love my womb and to embrace the art of menstruating well.

Blood Rites

We all need ritual, especially menstrual ritual. Menstruation calls for rituals of retreat and quietude. Inward journeying rituals, self-care rituals and dream work rituals are perfect for this part of a woman's cycle. Celebrate your miraculous creative nature by performing your own special blood rites. Here are a couple of rituals which I like to include in my moon-time.

Pre-Menstrual Bath

Make an infusion with 6 cups boiled water and the following herbs:

1/4 cup Roses, 1/4 cup Lavender, 1 cup Mugwort

Strain the infusion into your bath and enjoy in the days before your period.

Wise Woman Dream Tea

This is a special treat just for the premenstrual woman. Since it has emmenagogues in it, it should not be consumed at any other time of the month, or by women who suffer from particularly heavy or too frequent bleeding. It is not for pregnant women.

On the eve of your moon-time make an infusion of 1 tsp Rose buds, 3 Tbsp Mugwort, 1/2 tsp Lavender in a 4 cup teapot.

Enjoy the Pre-Menstrual Bath above and sip on the Wise Woman Dream Tea as you get ready for bed.

Ask your Guardians and Guides to visit you in the dream realm. Ask them to watch over, protect and inspire your dreams. Keep a journal by your bed in case you awaken with dreams to record.

Self Massage

You can perform this massage any time of the month, but go very gently over the uterus during menses, with the lightest touch. Spread a large towel on your bed and close the door. Play some soft music. Anoint your Goddess altar with the simple intention of feeling your feelings. Remove your clothes and begin in lotus pose. Using a natural oil (I like almond oil or coconut oil with a few drops of Lavender mixed in), massage your body, starting with your feet and moving up the shins and thighs. Massage up the legs to the abdomen. Lie back and massage very gently with sweeping clockwise motions around the navel. Emphasize what is felt inside as well as the touch itself. Close your eyes and feel the emotions inside, that which flows, that which is stuck. Continue moving your hands clockwise to encourage the flow of digestion. Stop and lightly rest your hands over your uterus and ovaries for a minute or so, just feeling inwards deeper and deeper. Move up to your breasts and massage in a circular motion. Move over the shoulder and down each arm to the hand then and work your way back up towards the heart. Finish up with gratitude for the connection you feel to your creative center.

Blood Offering

The first time I performed this ritual was by accident. I was on a secluded walk in nature, while menstruating. I had to pee and found a safe place to squat. While squatting I observed that a lot of blood also passed from my body into the earth and instantly disappeared. I received a surge of energy through my whole being and had the distinct impression that the earth actually drank my blood up with a great thirst. I sensed that it was only natural for my blood to return to Her, that I was instantly and deeply connected to the Goddess in this small yet vital offering. So, if you ever get the chance to let your blood flow directly into the earth, I encourage you to give it a try. See how it makes you feel.

In the years since that moment I've had the opportunity and curiosity to research different traditions of returning blood to the earth. I recently moved out of the city and finally have my own washing machine so I have started using organic cotton cloth pads which I soak in a bucket of water before washing. The blood and water from the soaking bucket are offered into my garden, connecting into the web of life all around me. Not only am I giving an offering to the earth and plants, but I am keeping disposables out of the landfill and no longer over-consuming cotton, plastic and paper materials associated with disposable pads and their packaging- this is a great feeling. There is power and continuity in putting some of myself into the herbs I grow and then taking those herbs into my body. Imagine how powerful the herbs are that grow outside of your door, nourished by your own creative blood. In reciprocity, you nourish them and then they nour- ish you, ad infinitum.

Yet another layer of this practice is that it calls me to be pure. One who is medicated, diseased or toxic should not share her blood into the earth. In this way the earth gently calls me to be my best self so that my blood is a worthy offering. I take no medications. My diet is clean. The products I use in my home, on my skin and in my garden are organic and non-toxic. The earth cares for me and I care for Her. Something lost is found. Something broken is whole again. This practice has healed me is ways I am only begin-ning to understand.

Tips: If this concept appeals to you, get yourself some organic cotton reusable pads. Place used pads in a bucket of cold water to soak. When you are ready to wash them, remove them from the bucket, and wring them out and offer the water into the garden. Give them a thorough second rinse and offer that water into the garden as well. Soak them for an hour in another bucket of water with two cups of white vinegar to one gallon of water, to sanitize. Wring out your pads and dump the vinegar and water solution down the toilet. Then machine wash your pads in cold water and hang to dry. If you grow food that you share with other people, they might prefer that you do not feed your blood to those plants. Feel free to share your blood with herbs grown for your own personal use as well as all plant beings not consumed by humans.

If you have your own garden you may want to have a special long flow-ing skirt or dress of dark color for your moon time. Put on your long flow-ing skirt and walk barefoot and without underwear into your garden. Squat close to the earth and make an offering of your sacred blood. Don't worry about making a mess. If your neighbors are around, pretend you are weed-ing. Rinse the blood into the earth with some water, if necessary.

Well Woman Womb Care

Herbal teas such as Raspberry Leaf, Nettle, Oatstraw and Rooibos can be enjoyed consistently throughout the month to keep the uterus toned, mineral levels (calcium, magnesium, potassium etc) abundant and hormones in balance. A few excellent diuretics and diaphoretics are Elder Flower, Dandelion Root and Burdock Root to help with bloating. Antispasmodics which can help prevent and treat cramps such as Nettle and Red Clover are staples for any woman's herbal cabinet. Chart your cycle with a Lunar Calendar. Tack it to your wall and mark each day of blood. Over time your personal blood pattern will emerge. It is remarkable to see and anticipate the rhythms of your own womb. This can also help you to address any imbalances or inconsistencies in your flow. You can practice self-massage which connects you to the uterus and acquaints you with all the many physical and emotional feelings within your core on any given day. Japanese Hara Massage or Mayan Abdominal Massage both can help rekindle awareness in the lower chakras (the root and the spleen). All forms of womb repression and stigmatization can alienate women from connecting lovingly to this sacred source. By performing self massage to this area we can restore our womb consciousness. The hands extend out of and are an important part of the heart chakra. When they connect with loving intention to the creative centers below, an instant sense of wholeness and self-knowledge emerge. This simple touch can unlock the power, the knowing, the rhythms, the emotional truths and the creativity held within the womb. Remember.

CHAPTER NINE

Self-Love

✦ ❦ ❦ ✦

Whether you are already great at taking care of your body or not, this chapter addresses some basic ideas on how to care for and nourish your sacred vessel so that it will function as its best, both as a spiritual channel and as a healthy container of pleasure and fulfillment. Spiritual growth springs forth from a well-loved, nourished, sensual, balanced body. Keep in mind that self-care is most possible when we come from a place of self-love.

Let thy food be thy Medicine

"Let thy food be thy medicine and thy medicine be thy food" is excellent advice from Hippocrates. As you grow more and more sensitive, you may want to bring greater intention to eating correctly. Eating healthfully in this day and age is equally about what you don't eat, as what you do eat. With the goal of treating the body as a sacred vessel you must choose your Goddess diet with care. Simplicity is best. You can avoid over-processed chemical and pesticide laden industrial foods by generally choosing whole, non-GMO, organic nutrition. Try growing some of your own food, even if only a pot of herbs or a jar of sprouts. Being in touch with where your sustenance comes from can be a very powerful experience. You could shop at a farmers' market or join a CSA. Go to an orchard or a berry patch and pick your own fruit. Contemplate "industrial food". Consider whether vegetarianism interests you, or at least where your meat comes from.

When you eat fish, fowl and meat, do your best to choose ethically hunted, fished, farmed and slaughtered animals. Eating animals that have been abused or raised in a toxic environment is not good for anyone: the animal, you, nor the environment "downstream" (which is in itself a dangerous myth). You might make friends with a hunter or become one. Or go fishing. Feel a part of the beautiful circle of life that is known as the food chain. When you do choose to eat red meat consider where in your menstrual cycle you are. The best times for a woman to eat red meat are just before, during or just after her period. Most of all, when you do eat fish, fowl or meat: be thankful for the life which was given. Feel worthy of the sacrifice.

Have you ever caught a big fish and fed your whole family with it? How about a bountiful harvest from your vegetable garden? Has a hunter in your family ever served you the most succulent cut of venison? Have you tasted cider made from your friend's apple trees? Did you ever make a pie from rhubarb you grew yourself? Connecting with where your food comes from and feeding your loved ones, provides a deep spiritual connection to the earth and an overwhelming gratitude for true sustenance.

Everything in Moderation

My mom raised us vegetarian. I am now a meat eater who still eats mostly vegetarian. I deny myself nothing, but restrict much. From my personal experience I have noticed that vegetarianism and meat eating create their own layers of consciousness and therefore can be used as tools to shift consciousness as needed. If I am feeling somewhat unreceptive, callous or coarsened and wish to refine my sensitivity I can become vegetarian for a time which amplifies the perceptions within the subtle body. I make the choice based on what I am going through and what will be required of me in body and spirit. Living in a densely populated corner of New England, for my body to stay healthy through the harsh winters, I make my immune boosting chicken soup about once a month. I frequently eat vegetarian for weeks on end but then if I feel the need for the strength and healing nourishment that can only be gotten from flesh and bone, then I will not deny myself. I will rejoice and be grateful for the life given to sustain mine. I feel worthy of whatever foods will give me the strength and fortitude required to continue on my path. My acupuncturist suggests eating red meat once a month around my period, but only once a month. I think this is good advice. "Everything in moderation" goes the Greek proverb.

The Kitchen Cauldron

Here are a few delicious and healing recipes you might like to cook up in your cauldron. Be aware that even organic, fresh herbs and veggies can be contraindicated for certain health conditions. For example, people who are taking blood thinners or are prone to blood clots should avoid leafy greens high in vitamin K (named for the word koagulant in German), such as kale, because of the active blood coagulant properties. Or pregnant women and women with short cycles or heavy menses, ought to minimize emmenagogues in their cooking, such as parsley. Knowledge is power. Know your body and know your food. Experiment. Enjoy nourishing and nurturing yourself, your friends and family from within your kitchen cauldron. Be empowered by the difference you can make in your own health and your family's health by cooking from scratch. There is almost nothing more grounding than cooking good wholesome food. I often receive my best ideas while in working in the kitchen.

SPRING NETTLE SOUP

One half pound fresh stinging nettles

One cup precooked fluffy white rice (Carolina or Basmati are good non-sticky options)

Four yellow onions chopped

Six cups mushroom vegetable broth (use broth recipe below- add shitake stems)

Salt and pepper

Olive oil

Butter

Ten Shitake Mushroom caps chopped

Spring nettles can be found in nature. You can plant them in your garden if you have one or you can find them at farmer's markets and health food stores. Nettle soup begins with the quest of acquiring the main ingredient. This is the first step of the journey. Harvesting them yourself is the most fun, but finding them at the farmer's market is also quite exciting!

Sautee the mushrooms in olive oil. Season with salt. Remove from the oil and set aside. Protecting your hands with gloves or plastic bags, rinse the nettles. Blanch them briefly (which removes the sting) and trim away any tough stems. Roughly chop nettles and set aside. Give thanks for the rare gift of tender, tonifying spring nettles. Bring broth to a simmer. Gently brown the onions in olive oil and butter in a soup pot. Add simmering broth, rice and nettles to the soup pot. Simmer gently for a few minutes. Remove soup from heat. Allow to cool a bit before blending thoroughly. The soup should have a very fine blended texture. Season with salt and pepper to taste. Serve piping hot with chopped shitakes sprinkled on top.

BROTH

Keep a bag in the freezer for vegetable trimmings: celery, onion, garlic, carrots, mushroom stems, parsley stems, fennel fronds. You can utilize these scraps in whatever broth you are preparing.

If you don't have a full bag of frozen trimmings on hand, roughly chop an onion, a couple of carrots, garlic cloves, celery stalks and leaves. Add veggies to the pot, plus a bay leaf, a couple of pepper corns, a pinch of coriander and a tiny pinch of anise seed.

Feel free to add some dried Reishi, Turmeric or Astragalus from your medicine cabinet.

Add water to cover well. Simmer for a half hour. Strain and salt to taste.

If you want to make it a bone broth, add chicken bones and thyme. Simmer for a couple of hours.

CONGEE

1 cup brown rice

6 cups water

2 inch chunk of fresh ginger root, peeled

Salt

Sesame oil

3 stalks celery chopped

2 carrots diced

1 onion finely chopped

10 shitake mushroom caps chopped

Soy sauce

Combine rice, water, ginger root and a pinch of salt in a sauce pan and bring to a boil. Reduce flame and simmer for a half hour or so. While the rice is simmering, cook the carrots, celery, mushrooms and onion in sesame oil in a skillet over a low heat.

When the rice thickens to porridge consistency it is about done cooking. Add the veggies to the rice and stir. Add sesame oil, black pepper and soy sauce to taste. Remove from the heat and serve.

Congee is an easy to digest, nutritious rice porridge. It is great for anyone recovering from an illness, or suffering from poor digestion. It's also good as a part of a cleansing diet. Congee is a perfect food to eat if you are coming off of a fast as well.

ROASTED ACORN SQUASH SOUP

2 medium acorn squash

2 onions finely chopped

Fresh thyme

1 quart of vegetable broth

1 teaspoon of ground sumac (available at Middle Eastern specialty food stores)

Salt and pepper

Olive oil

1 Tablespoon of butter

Preheat oven to 350 degrees. Cut the squash in half to remove the seeds. Place fleshy side down on an oiled baking sheet. Bake until the flesh is soft and slightly caramelized but not burnt.

Lightly brown the onions in olive oil. Add about a teaspoon of fresh thyme leaves. Add the butter and continue cooking over low heat. Scoop the flesh of the squash into the soup pot, being careful not to include any shreds of the tough outer skin. Add the broth and ground sumac. Bring to a gentle simmer and then remove from the heat. Allow the soup to cool a bit before blending. Add salt and pepper to taste. Serve hot.

DANDELION GREENS LASAGNA

1 box lasagna noodles, parboiled

1 bunch of dandelion green tops, finely chopped

16 oz whole milk ricotta

One cup grated Parmigiano Regiano

16 oz fresh mozzarella (8 oz thinly sliced for the top, 8 oz shredded)

32 oz marinara sauce

1 egg, beaten

1 cup fresh Italian parsley chopped

Salt and pepper

Preheat oven to 375 degrees. Combine egg, ricotta, parmigiano, parsley, dandelion greens and shredded mozzarella in a bowl. Spoon marinara into the lasagna dish to lightly cover the bottom. Place a layer of parboiled noodles followed by cheese and greens mixture. Salt and pepper. Repeat layers until dish is full. Layer remaining mozzarella over the top and loosely cover with foil. Bake for a half hour and uncover. Bake another 15 minutes or until top is lightly browned.

CHICKEN SOUP

1 Tbsp Turmeric

Half cup dried Reishi

One bunch Fresh Thyme

Four Bay leaves

Eight chicken thighs

Eight carrots

One heart of Celery sliced

One cup white or brown rice cooked al dente

One cup wild rice cooked al dente

Two onions chopped

One head garlic chopped

Salt and pepper

Olive oil

Place the chicken in the pot. Place a few sprigs of fresh thyme and two bay leaves in the pot. Give thanks for the chickens whose lives were sacrificed. Take a moment to get in touch with gratitude. Roughly chop one onion, three carrots, half a head of garlic, the trimmed ends and leaves of celery, plus the outer stalks, and add to pot. Fill with water to cover well and add the turmeric and a tsp salt. Bring to a boil and reduce to a simmer. After an hour add reishi and two more sprigs of thyme.

In a second soup pot, lightly brown one onion, finely chopped, in olive oil. Add remaining garlic, celery and peeled and chopped carrots plus two more bay leaves. Once the broth has been simmering an hour and a half check the chicken. When the meat is falling off the bone remove the chicken from the pot. Strain the broth into the second soup pot. Carefully remove the meat from the bones and add to the soup. Add cooked white and wild rice. Simmer gently a few minutes. Salt and pepper to taste. Strip all remaining thyme leaves from the sprigs and serve each bowl of chicken soup with a half tsp of the fresh thyme.

KALE POTATO GRATIN

½ bunch kale, cleaned, trimmed and chopped

6 potatoes, parboiled and sliced

1 onion, finely chopped

1 head garlic, chopped

Olive oil

1 pound gruyere shredded

1 cup white wine

Salt and pepper

Preheat oven to 375 degrees. Oil a casserole dish. Place a layer of potatoes, followed by onions and garlic, followed by kale, followed by salt and pepper, followed by gruyere. Repeat until casserole is full. Sprinkle remaining cheese on the top. Pour wine evenly over the top. Drizzle with olive oil. Bake covered with foil for a half hour. Uncover the gratin and allow to bake until the top is slightly browned.

VEGETABLE FRIED RICE

1 cup brown or white rice cooked

3 broccoli crowns cut in bite-size pieces

3 large carrots sliced

10 shitake mushroom caps chopped

4 stalks of celery chopped

1 onion finely chopped

4 cloves garlic minced

2 inches of ginger root peeled and finely chopped

1 cup peas (fresh or frozen)

1 large egg

Coconut oil

Sesame oil

Soy sauce

Rice vinegar

In a large skillet or wok gently brown onions in coconut oil over a low flame. Add mushrooms celery and garlic. Add broccoli, carrots and ginger root. Sparingly pour soy sauce, rice vinegar and sesame oil over the top and cover, allowing the vegetables to steam without burning. When the vegetables are cooked and seasoned to your liking add the rice to the skillet as well. Add peas. Bring the heat up to medium. Create a clearing in the center and crack and egg into a drop of hot sesame oil. Beat the egg with a fork as you gradually stir the rice and veggies into the egg, evenly distributing the egg throughout. Cover and allow the egg to be cooked by the hot steam for a few minutes. Stir again and check the flavor- add more soy sauce to taste and possibly more sesame oil. Enjoy!

WINTER SALAD

Combine fresh rosemary and balsamic vinegar in a pan. Reduce the vinegar on the stovetop. Whisk with a fresh crushed and chopped clove of garlic with salt, olive oil, a bit of anchovy paste and lemon zest.

Toss with baby arugula, roasted pecans, fresh pomegranate (sliced pear, persimmon or roasted beets will also do) and crumbled blue cheese

SUMMER SALAD

One whole Persian cucumber peeled and diced. One quarter of a red onion minced. Quarter cup of chopped fresh parsley. Quarter cup of chopped fresh mint. Half teaspoon of dried oregano. Half teaspoon sumac. Lightly dress with olive oil and red wine vinegar. Toss and salt and pepper to taste.

Fasting and Cleansing

Fasting and cleansing can be a part of a quiet retreat; a time to bathe, to rest and move slowly, a time of self-care and re-centering. Many favor spring and fall for a fast. Often people have emotional, even spiritual break-throughs while fasting. If you do choose to fast or cleanse make sure that you tailor all your life plans to fit your body's needs.

Fasting gives the digestive tract a much needed break. By letting the digestive system have some time off for a few days, a lot of energy is freed up to perform the work of maintenance and replenishment on a cellular level. No longer busy digesting and metabolizing, the organs of elimination and detoxification can perform deeper self-cleaning and self-healing than is normally possible. This can make you look luminous and feel great, often surprisingly energetic and light.

Avoid relying on sugary drinks or caffeine for energy while fasting. Instead go for fresh vegetable juices and nice homemade nourishing broths when you are feeling hungry. Drink plenty of water and herbal teas. If necessary, while fasting you can allow some foods that don't require chewing if you feel you really need or want to- such as kefir, pureed cooked vegetables or a smoothie.

Ease into a fast by first eliminating toxins and following a cleansing diet for at least a week prior. When your fast is finished ease back out of it with simple easy to digest foods such as soup and rice porridge (see congee recipe above). If you feel a fast would do you good, do it at a time when you can stay close to home or go into a retreat space. Start small with a one to three day fast in the spring or fall. Prepare plenty of blood sugar stabilizing teas, such as burdock or dandelion root tea. Prepare fresh bone broth or miso broth to keep on hand and heat up on the stove. Hot liquids are perfect for fasting. Drink tea all day and have some broth. Have a nice fresh raw vegetable juice as well. Or even a delicious fruit juice.

Bath Recipes and Rituals

Bathing is one of the quickest, easiest, most accessible ways to shift consciousness. You simply feel different after a bath (or a shower, or a swim for that matter) than you did before. The power of water is not to be underestimated. Heal yourself, cleanse yourself and transform yourself with sacred water. We generally bathe to cleanse our bodies, but our minds and our spirits are also profoundly affected by this cleansing process. If you brew up some tea for your bath, make it extra strong as it will be diluted once you strain it into your bath water.

RELEASING AND PURIFICATION BATH

Make an infusion with 6 cups boiled water and the following herbs:

2 tbsp Comfrey

1/2 cup Lavender

1/2 cup Nettles

Strain the infusion into your bath and enjoy. To add an extra layer of psychic cleansing add a ½ cup of sea salt to the bath.

HAIR AND SKIN BATH

Make an overnight infusion of 6 cups boiled water and the following herbs:

1/4 cup Burdock Root

1/4 cup Chrysanthemum

1/2 cup Mugwort

2 Tablespoons Elder Flower

1/4 cup Nettle

Strain the infusion into your bath and enjoy. Add a cup of unpasteurized cider vinegar to soften skin, encourage healthy pH balance, add shine to hair among other benefits. Once your hair and skin dry, the vinegar smell completely dissipates.

RELAXATION BATH

Make an infusion of 6 cups boiled water and the following herbs:

1/2 cup Lavender

1/2 cup Chrysanthemum

1 cup Mugwort

Strain the infusion into your bath and enjoy.

SALT AND MINERAL BATHS

Magically salt has grounding properties; the ability to absorb psychic energy and draw it back to the earth. Sea salts are nice for baths as they also impart minerals as well as psychic cleansing. For physical healing Dead Sea salts are known to provide relief from many ailments due to their particular mineral content. Magnesium rich Epsom salts are good for the body. You can add baking soda or cider vinegar if the salt you have on hand is drying to your skin.

Sacred Waters

What better way to celebrate the sacred live giving waters of Earth than to make a pilgrimage to a natural hot spring? There are so many amazing hot springs to explore. Here are three of my favorites…

Ojo Caliente- Truly sacred and rejuvenating waters. People have been bathing in this spot for thousands of years. Ojo Caliente is in the high desert of New Mexico between Santa Fe and Taos. Many luxury spa and hotel amenities are available as well as RV camping hookups. Bathing suits required.

Breitenbush- High in the mountains of Oregon, Breitenbush can only be reached in the warm season. A true detoxification environment in every way- no electronics allowed, leave your phone, watch and tablet in the car. The cabins have no electricity, so it's bed time once the sun goes down. Look for the giant stone Medicine Wheel set into the river bank. The dining hall provides delicious home grown healthy fare. Clothing optional while bathing.

Terwilliger Hot Springs at Cougar Dam- About an hour daytrip from Eugene, Oregon, this place is volunteer maintained and down a dirt hiking trail into the woods about a quarter of a mile. The spring comes out of a cave hot and feeds into a series of pools that cascade into one another, each one successively cooler. There is a box for donations to help maintain the trail and pools. Clothing optional.

Salt of the Earth

At both Ojo Caliente and Breitenbush I had similar experiences after bathing which involved sleeping for about sixteen hours, to wake feeling as if I'd been asleep for a thousand years, utterly rejuvenated. While I'm not exactly sure of the mineral analysis at either hot spring, my belief is that both springs are particularly high in Lithia. Lithia is a salt which humans need for balanced brain chemistry. We are supposed to get this naturally from our water supply, but nowadays there are so many pollutants in our water that most towns have to filter the water very thoroughly which also removes the good minerals we need as well as the toxins. In my family there is a history of manic depression so I am interested in natural ways of balancing mental health. I've been to many hot springs, but it is the lithia-rich springs which impact me most profoundly.

For example at Breitenbush, my husband and I had a pool to ourselves. We soaked for a while along the banks of the river. Then we wandered through a medicine wheel made of rocks set into the earth, feeling quite stoned somehow from our soak as the sun sparkled off the rushing rapids. When the sun went down we fell asleep in our cabin planning to wake with the breakfast bell. When the bell rang we awoke, but it turned out to be the lunch bell- we had slept sixteen hours without stirring and both felt as fresh as daisies, renewed and replenished.

Rest and Replenish

Being awake is not more important than sleeping, just like the full moon is not more important than the dark moon. They are equally important. We need more sleep during the long nights of winter and less with the long days of the summer. We also need more sleep than men. If we give our bodies exactly what they need, they begin to function at a very high level. If we tune our instruments with love and care they become so sensitive that we can begin to navigate with more mastery. Sleep is not something to be rushed. Our dreaming minds are equally, if not more fruitful than our waking minds. Prepare for a night's sleep with the same attention you bring to the day's tasks. If you sleep well, you will wake well.

Cultivating a rich sleeping life is essential to maintaining real balance. When you are properly rested your dreams become a channel for Divine transmissions. When you are replenished, peace and clarity come easily in waking life. If you would like to improve your sleep, start with letting yourself feel tired at bedtime. Avoid caffeine beyond morning hours (or completely). Make your bedroom a retreat space - no phones, digital clocks, TVs, tablets- nothing that will beep or glow in the dark and distract you from the important undoing of sleep. If you have to deal with light or sound pollution, consider adding a white noise source or blackout curtains. Make an effort to go to bed earlier.

Create a special bedtime ritual that helps you unwind and look forward to crawling into bed. Make sure your bed is comfortable and has soft clean sheets. Invest in PJs that make you feel comfortable and cozy. Climbing into a nicely made bed after a long day and a hot bath is a wonderful way to wind down. A good book and a cup of tea, also help to relax. Treat yourself like you would a little child at bedtime- give yourself a bath, get your jammies on, read some bedtime stories and have a cup of chamomile tea- what worked when you were a little girl, still works today! There are multiple herbs listed in the herbal compendium which help calm the nerves, promote sleep and enhance dreams.

Deeper Sanctuary

Retreats are another way of replenishing the body, mind and spirit. Getting away from responsibilities and workaday habits allows us to go deep within and find the center once again. If your life is fast paced, citi-fied, plugged-in; if your candle burns at both ends; if you give everything you have to taking care of others, or if you've been through a major loss, sickness or trauma you might be due for a retreat. Retreats can involve fast-ing, silent meditation, ritual cleansing, gentle yoga, healing touch, spiritual journeying and emotional purging. A retreat can involve community or be solitary in nature. Doing a retreat that also has an element of pilgrimage is particularly powerful.

Whether your travel thousands of miles to a pristine natural hot spring or retreat within an urban oasis, your sacred space should be devoid of obligations, stressors and distractions (TV, phone, computer) to allow the important work of replenishment to become the focus. It's ideal to go into a secluded place of retreat in nature, but if that's not immediately practical, you can also create a weekend retreat within your own home, with some careful planning.

Or you can always take a simple five minute break to rest and replen-ish, such as the following grounding ritual. Find your sanctuaries, large and small as frequently as possible.

Lie on the Ground

Weather permitting, find a piece of earth to lie down on. It could be in your garden, at the beach or under a tree in your local park. Take your shoes off and let the soles of your feet touch the earth. Lie back on the ground with knees bent and palms down. Close your eyes and do some deep releasing exhales to clear your energy. Breathe gently and deeply for a couple of minutes. Relax into the strong solid Earth. Let Her hold and soothe your energy. Allow Her to pull anything from you that no longer serves. Feel it leave your body as you give it to the earth. Stay here until you feel your energy stabilize and recharge. Move onto your hands and knees. Bow to the earth and give Her a kiss.

You are the Weaver

We have already covered many topics, with more to come. Please take time to integrate any new ideas you are implementing. Pace yourself and if you are making changes consider making just one at a time rather than trying to do it all at once. It can be overwhelming to reweave everything at the same time. Let your transformation be gentle and slow.

Start with the thing that feels the most urgent and once you get the hang of that particular new pattern in your life, then you will know when you are ready to weave another new pattern in your tapestry. This is joyful, beautiful and deep work, so remind yourself to take your time and enjoy the upgrades. If you start to get information overload that is a sign that what you've already taken in needs to be integrated before you can absorb anymore.

There is much to be unraveled before it can be rewoven in the pattern of your choosing. You are the Weaver. You are the Meaning-Maker. You are weaving a whole world and it is a huge undertaking! Be patient with yourself and pay attention to where your self-care energy wants to go. There are no mistakes. Unravel and reweave as many times as you like, Creatrix.

Self-Care Prayer

Goddess, God, Angels, Guardians, and Guides: Please open my heart to feel the self-love, self-worth and self-kindness required to practice self-care. Please make me wise so that I may discern what is needed physically in order to be centered emotionally and spiritually. Please give me the power to follow through with the self-care I need to live my best life. Thank you. I love you.

CHAPTER TEN
Centering

❖⤜⟋∼⟍⤛❖

By embracing your spiraling, cyclical, interior nature, your confidence, power and ability to manifest outwardly grow. Use circular symbols to enhance the power and mythology of your own Sacred Center. Only by being centered can we truly know our purpose on earth. When we live from our innermost power, we feel safe, secure and at home in our skin. If we occupy that sacred space within, we are more able to share our gifts with the world without.

Coven

Finding the right spiritual community for you is something that might happen once you've developed a strong foundation within your own intuition. Once that base is fully formed you can trust that you will make good choices and you'll be able to tune into the right people for you. Grow your community slowly, organically and intuitively, starting with experienced teachers and healers. Bring gifted empathic humans into your innermost circle. Let them guide you and heal you. Seek out trustworthy teachers who can show you the way to journey with spirit in safe and protected ways. When you are with the right people the earth will feel solid beneath you. You will feel held in a warm embrace.

As you develop your ritual consciousness, invite likeminded friends into your circle. There are group classes and gatherings offered to the public in the backrooms of crystal shops and esoteric bookstores. There are increasing numbers of women's retreats which allow for deep awakening of sisterhood. Check them out with a discerning mind and an open heart. You may have gifts that you want to share with community. As you grow and heal you may likely need to be seen and heard by others who are walking a similar path as you. Your people are out there and they need you the same way you need them. It is a joyful homecoming to find your people and to be able to stand in your spiritual truth openly with support. There in that circle you are seen and you are held, and you see and you hold. This is your coven.

Take stock of your inner and outer circles; the people in your life. It is important that all of these relationships are based on mutual integrity, trust, respect and admiration. You are a sensitive being who can only blossom in full love and light. Spend your days with the people who bring you up, make you feel light and free. Spend your precious time with people who accept and love you for who you are. Your gifts are meant to be shared with those who are able to receive them. You deserve to have loving Friends, Family, Teachers, Healers, Spirit Guides, Guardian Angels, Goddesses and Gods in your circle. You deserve companions with whom you can laugh and cry. Fill your circle with those who will grow with you along your spiritual path. The people in your circle should understand and support you and all you are becoming. This is your choice and your responsibility; your coven.

Witch is the Word

In my book, a witch is an empowered woman; a woman in tune with all of nature; a woman as free as the wind and as rooted as a great oak. She is a Sister, a Healer, a Creatrix, a Priestess, a Seer, a Shadow Walker, a Dreamer, a Weaver, a Divine Channel, a Wise Woman and Mistress of her own Destiny. Just as we reclaim the symbols of the Goddess there is power in reclaiming this word: Witch. This sacred word is yours. Whether you choose to shout it from a mountain top, embroider it on the inside of your cloak or simply whisper it into the darkness, it is your sacred word to use as you wish. Call yourself what you will Sister: Priestess, Sorceress, Healer, Witch. You are seen and you are known in the darkness and light. Your wounds are shared by all women. Your strength and your magic will never die. Stand firm at your cauldron, under the full moon, in this great Goddess garden and root deeply into this ancient sisterhood. In this secret circle of love and mystery, the gate stands ajar. Kindly welcome your sisters to warm themselves by the fire, for yours is the power of the Gatekeeper.

The Sacred Swirl

The symbolic cauldron describes the principles of Expression and Creation as yet another form of Alchemy. By embracing the power of your own mind over matter, you activate and amplify your magical abilities. By believing the most powerful beliefs you become your most empowered self. We each have all kinds of purpose. The cauldron calls us to create our creations, to allow our ideas to bubble and swirl. It calls us to honor the sacred creative center embodied by the hearth fire and the abundant vessel. The cauldron reveals the mystical creative power in all women. It represents the womb and the creative potential therein. It also represents the mind, the heart, the soul; all of our creative parts. Just as Gaia birthed herself from the swirling womb of Chaos, we are all essentially and inherently creative. There is so much which needs expression within this cauldron. We each are urged to express and create many things in our lifetimes.

You might be called to sing a song, record it and perform it in front of many people. Your path might lead you to have children and create a home for them. You might be moved to make healing herbal infusions. You might have something to say, a story to share, a message for the people. You could express yourself through dance or performance art. Or perhaps your

113

mission is to create community or connect through humanitarianism or environmental activism. You might be called to build a business or three. You may be on a healing path. Whatever it is that makes your cauldron swirl, this is what the world wants from you.

The cauldron is first and foremost overflowing with self-creativity, self-expression and self-healing. The cauldron brings forth from its psychic depths: big ideas, nourishing broths, magical solutions, medicinal cures, loving abundance. Just like Goddess Cerridwen, own your cauldron and occupy your creative center. Stir it, stoke it, simmer it, spice it. Eat and be nourished from it. Taste the flavors within. Be guided by the inner senses and intuition. Speak your truth. Paint your pictures. Dance your dance.

If the system you are in is broken, make your own system. Become a whole new kind of Gatekeeper. If the well is poisoned, take your divining rod and go find a new source. Be empowered by taking a stand. Free thinking is magic. Create yourself and create your life. Your cauldron has many secrets to teach you. There is much for you to create, good that you can do in the world and many hearts you will touch when you bring forth from your sacred cauldron.

Anneke's Cauldron

My mom is an Artist and an Activist. She's a Shiatsu therapist, a retired Nurse and a self-taught Herbalist. She has the greenest thumb in town. She's been arrested countless times for her environmental activism against Vermont Yankee, the nuclear plant upriver from my hometown. The nuclear plant was built on the Connecticut River in order to use the water as its cooling system.

It is directly because of grass-roots activists like my mom, that recently the nuclear plant was finally shut down. The first time my mom was arrested and incarcerated for protesting Vermont Yankee was 39 years ago. I was only a few months old at the time.

The winter following the closure of Vermont Yankee, the Connecticut River froze for the first time in forty years. My magical and powerful mother had a hand in that. She made the river freeze. That beautiful river which we were never allowed to swim in, for fear of radiation, can now begin to heal.

The Serpentine Coil

The spiral is yet another ancient circular symbol reminding us to go to the center. Representative of the Goddess and the womb, the spiral takes us ever deeper into the center of our being. The infinite universe goes unendingly outwards, and also unendingly inwards. As always, the microcosm reflects the macrocosm: as above, so below. By constantly seeking the center of our own being we gain access to the larger truths of the Divine. Ouroboros is another alchemical symbol of infinite nature; the serpent forms a perfect circle, seemingly biting its own tail. It gives birth to itself- it is self-created. Here again, our power to affect destiny increases, when we cycle ever deeper within ourselves.

Heart-Womb Healing

Write a letter from your sacred womb (your uterus, cervix, fallopian tubes and eggs) to yourself. Maybe it's a love letter. Maybe it's a letter full of secrets you've kept from yourself. Maybe it's a letter of forgiveness, grief or rage. Only the womb knows. Put it in a self-addressed, stamped envelope. Take it to a mailbox and drop it in.

When you receive this letter read it carefully. From the compassionate heart space of unconditional love, write a letter back to your womb. Put it in a self-addressed, stamped envelope. Take it to a mailbox and drop it in.

When you receive the letter, carefully read it from the perspective of your womb center. Take some time to sit with, feel into and process the heart-womb connection.

Place one hand on your heart center and the other hand on your womb center. Breathe.

Say aloud "I forgive and I am forgiven. I love and I am loved. I know and I am known. I accept and I am accepted. I feel and I am felt. I hold and I am held. I heal and I am healed."

Breathe and allow any emotions that surface to flow freely.

Practice self-care afterwards- a simple cup of tea, an herbal bath, a yoga session, a walk in the woods or time alone to journal.

The goal of this ritual is to foster an enhanced compassionate connection between the heart and the womb. Keep these letters on file to tap back into where you were when you did this ritual and feel free to repeat the ritual in the future to see how your heart-womb relationship has healed and grown over time.

PART III
BELOVED WITCH

CHAPTER ELEVEN

Darkness and Lightness

As you develop your powers and expand your connected conscious-ness, you will become more able to face and heal what hides in your shadows. As the light within you grows, you will learn to shine it into the darkest most sorrowful corners of your psyche and that of the collec-tive consciousness. From within your sacred circle, you will bear witness. Accept what lives in the shadows with compassion and love, even as you choose to walk in the light and move towards the good and the sweet. Tune your sensitive receiver to the Love and Light channel without turning your back on the wound.

As you heal yourself and become more masterful at taking care of your own energy field, you will have more healing power to share, more love to give, more light to shine. As you traverse the psychic depths, embrace the darkness of night, the dark moon and the inner truths of the subconscious mind. It is within the darkness that secrets are revealed. Be willing to face your own shadows, to move within them, to know yourself and heal.

The Truth Seeker within faces into experience and transforms through it. Use the myriad Goddess aspects available within you to understand the true nature of all phenomena and how to grow. Occult guidance will help lead you through the shadows. Use every tool you have to create your Sacred Center, to build an inviolate vessel and an illuminated pathway into the crystal temple wherein you dance your dreams and work your magic. You are weaving your life out of shadows and light, love and pure intention.

Shadow Woods Meditation

Come to a comfortable seated or reclining position where you will not be disturbed. Invoke the Divine Ones to hold the space for your healing visualization. Take your time to enter into a meditative state by slowing and deepening your breath. Visualize a forest in your mind's eye. There is a soft dirt path among the trees. Walk down the path.

Under the canopy of the forest there are many shadows. These are your shadows. There is the shadow of the thing that you wanted but did not get. There is the shadow of a part of yourself that was taken from you. There is a dream you abandoned by the wayside. These shadows hang among the trees like Spanish moss. Touch them. Feel them. Remember them. Walk softly among your shadows. Be comfortable with them. Observe and recognize each one swaying in the breeze. Take your time here with each shadow and let the feelings arise.

When you are ready, continue walking down the path towards a clearing. As you step out of the woods the sun envelops you in pure blinding light. Open your eyes and briefly journal about each shadow you encountered. Give thanks to your Spirit Allies.

If there are parts of you which you've lost but would like to reconnect to, invite them to come home. Place some flowers upon your altar for them. In time, see what happens. If there were shadows of disappointments look back and see if there was any kind of silver lining to not getting that thing you wanted. If there were any abandoned dreams, ask yourself if that is still a dream of yours or is there a new dream. Take stock of these shadows. They are yours. They want a little bit of attention. There may be healing or growth opportunities in those dark shadowy woods.

Mistress of Her Own Shadows

Shadow work is anything that embraces, expresses and heals the shadow. There is a misconception that spiritual people must live in the light all of the time. Everybody has a dark side and it must be expressed. Healthy expression of the darkness is in my opinion a spiritual practice. It is an expression of healing and self-love. It acknowledges the places you've been, the wounds you carry and the worthiness of your voice. Whatever you have lived through and the ways you have survived deserve to be honored and respected. At times the shadow wants to be seen, heard and witnessed. I promise you that healthy expression of the shadow makes room for more and more lightness in your heart.

Learn to love the Devil inside. Pay attention to her and give her what she needs. She sometimes just needs a safe space to rage- like the edge of a mosh pit or in front of a blank canvas, for example. Sometimes she needs to howl at the moon and shake her fist at the sky. Sometimes she just needs to weep and cry out "Why God, why?" Hold her like a child. Make safe spaces for her wailing. This is the work of Spirit. Goddess and God, Angels, Guardians and Guides are all with you there in those shadows. Your darkness is full of love and healing.

The impulse to destroy is always a potential where there has been trauma, but it can be channeled in ways that cause harm to none. The feelings of rage, pain, fear, grief and betrayal that can result from abandonment, neglect, abuse, poverty, oppression and violence- these emotions cannot be suppressed. When you have this kind of energy surging through you, you have no choice but to master your shadows, to express them, to find your way in and out of the darkness. There is truly no viable alternative.

What I call the Devil here is any aspect of self that acts out to bring attention to a wound. This could be your Inner Child, a grieving Maiden or Mother aspect, or a traumatized Inner Guardian perhaps. It could need expression through art, exorcism through ritual, healing from the earth, fortification through learning self-defense, nurturing by being held in community, or all of the above. Love this Devil for she holds the key to your wholeness and healing. Give her expression. Go unfettered and fearlessly into her shadows.

Rainbow Journey

Does your Inner Child need some attention? Build a circular Goddess altar out of flowers, herbs and crystals. Include any offerings you suspect your inner child might appreciate. Invoke the light as you sit in lotus pose in the center. Close your eyes and begin with slow, deep breath. Breathe gently, expanding and contracting. On each inhale allow your lungs to fill all the way to the top with air. Gently exhale until your lungs are completely empty on each exhale. As you deepen your breath, notice any tension you may be holding in your body. Send the energy of each inhale to those tense or tender areas in the body. With each exhale allow the tension to flow out.

As you enter into a relaxed state, begin to root down through your sacrum, sending glowing red roots down to the earth's core. With each inhale energy is stimulated. The root chakra is the center of identity, sexuality, foundations and "roots". There is a sense of being nourished and supported by Mother Earth. Feel you roots providing a strong foundation as you send them down deep.

With the next inhale pull energy up from earth's core and fill the spleen center with deep orange light. Let the breath activate the swirling cauldron of the spleen chakra. This is your center of creative impulses, instinct, preservation and assimilation. Use the breath to swirl any impurities up and out.

On your next inhale, this energy rises into the golden radiant light of the solar plexus chakra. This is the center of personal dynamism, will power, achievement and true knowing. With each inhale the light of the sun shines brighter within the chakra. With each exhale shadows are cleared from within.

Fill your lungs to the top as the energy rises again into the whirling green wheel of the heart chakra. Exhale any pain from the heart chakra, the center of the higher self, psychic healing, love and compassion. Feel how expansive this center is, extending out and connecting into the web of Life.

With the next inhale allow the energy to ascend into the spinning ethereal pale turquoise light of the throat chakra. This chakra holds your emotions, self-expression and discernment. Allow your breath to move the energy through the throat chakra catching and removing toxins.

As the energy rises again it moves easily up to the royal blue light of the third eye. The chakra sparkles like a sapphire, the home of intuition, beckoning towards expanded consciousness - the Gateway to second sight.

On your next inhale the energy flows up again. You feel the violet light gently pop through your crown chakra, as a shimmering amethyst vapor rises towards heaven. The crown chakra is the center of Divine Unity and spiritual attainment. Continue breathing deeply as you simultaneously root down and flow up in perfect balance.

Begin to visualize a rainbow. In your vision, the rainbow comes down from the sky and through the walls of your room and envelops you in radiance, in synch with the rainbow of your chakras. Allow the rainbow to lift you up and transport you up into the sky, away from your body, your home, your town, above the clouds, through the stratosphere, out past the moon. The rainbow carries you back down again through the stratosphere and the clouds and gently sets you under a great holy tree. You find yourself in a safe, happy place. Only good things can happen here as you continue to breathe deeply and easily.

You notice a path which leads to a beautiful garden. You walk up to the gate and look into the sacred garden. You open the gate and step inside. You see a child playing in the garden. This child is an aspect of you. You observe her mood, appearance, activity. What is she doing? Does she see you? Maybe you have an interaction. Maybe she shows you something or gives you a sign or even a gift. Or maybe you have something that you would like to give to your Inner Child.

When you are ready to journey back home wave good bye to your Inner Child. Go back out the gate and walk back down the path to the great tree. As the rainbow descends again from the sky you are ensconced in radiant light and transported up again into the sky, out beyond the moon and back down through the atmosphere to earth. The rainbow delivers you back into your body. As you settle into your body continue to breathe fully and slowly. Allow all your chakras to gently retract into the self.

You can use the Rainbow Journey to go and visit any other aspects of self that need attention or that might have wisdom to offer. Perhaps you'd like to pay a visit to your Maiden, Mother, Crone or Inner Guardian.

I practiced the Inner Child meditation recently and was amused to see that my Inner Child was a wild feral thing. She came out of a cottage and ran around the garden. She began digging in the dirt with purpose and passion. There were all the usual creepy crawlies teeming within the earth. She was not so interested in them as she was in digging. She dug deeper. Beneath many layers of decaying and regenerating earth was a pure wellspring. Dig deeper. Get dirty. Make a mess. Dig. This is what she told me without saying a word.

The Space of your Sacred Sovereign Self

Healthy boundaries are strong and secure, yet flexible and adaptable. If your boundaries feel rigid, brittle or cracked they could possibly use some restorative work. You might often feel put upon or depleted from interacting with certain people. You might not notice that someone is encroaching upon your territory until they are already trespassing inside the gate.

If these kinds of feelings are being triggered, something in you needs to be held and protected. These feelings and situations are calling you to give tender loving care to your edges. Cultivate safe secure spaces. For a time, practice saying "no" more than you say "yes". Do less and be more in your safe space. Let your world be small. Pull your edges in and hold them strong like a cocoon. Feel that centered and contained feeling. Be empowered by your ability to delineate your boundaries and to simply choose to occupy the Space of your Sacred Sovereign Self.

Get in touch with what a strong negative response really feels like deep inside your body. Get in touch with what a strong affirmative response feels like inside your body. Feel the "NO!" and the "YES!" and then refine that awareness down to the smaller yeses, nos and everything in between. Bring consciousness into the physical, allowing this feeling and self-knowledge to grow your intuition and use it to flex and expand your boundaries, when you feel ready. As you gain power from this inner discernment, you will become more impervious to energetic invaders because the boundary will come to rest exactly where you need it to be, because it is coming directly from the source of your inner sovereignty.

It may take some time to let yourself be guided by what is known in your body. Check in regularly with your boundaries. See if they feel good, if they're in the right place, or if they are in need of adjustment. Cultivate this consciousness with practice and let it expand out to hold the sacred space of you. You have the power to adjust, protect and communicate your boundaries, guided by the truths held within your emotional body.

Unhooking Ritual

There are energetic connections between you and every single person who has touched your life, for better or for worse. Even if you haven't seen or spoken to an individual for decades that connection still exists. You may be leaking energy through these connections and giving power away that you are not even aware of. Or you may project your desires upon another individual, thus obscuring your view of that person's true nature or role in your life. This ritual enables you to sever harmful or debilitating energetic connections as well as remove illusory projections around your relationships.

Make a mental list of the individuals or relationships you would like to focus on. In the beginning you might think of just a few people. Over time you may perform this ritual over and over. Eventually you may unhook energetic connections with dozens of people. With each unhooking comes healing, restored strength and clarity.

Visualize your chakras or psychic centers. Each one houses different character traits and energies. For example, the solar plexus is the center which houses Psychic knowing, the power of the Will, personal dynamism and achievement. Imagine how it negatively affects your will-power, personal dynamism, ability to achieve and trust in psychic intuition, if people who have hurt you in the past are still energetically hooked into and draining this particular chakra.

You will need sage, a bar of soap and water. If you have access to a fire pit that is ideal. If not, this ritual can be performed in a bathroom or near a natural body of water. As with all releasing rituals this should be performed during the waning of the moon.

First smudge your chakras with sage. Invoke the highest love and light. Ask Archangels Michael and Raphael for assistance. Ask your guardians for guidance and protection. Locate north, south, east and west. Face in the direction of the person you wish to release. If you have a fire pit, put the fire between yourself and the one who is to be released. Visualize the individual, let him or her come into focus. Now see the energetic cord connecting you. Have a good look at this binding element. Notice what it looks like, how heavy it is, what it is made of. Observe where it comes to hook into you. What does the hook look like? How big is it? What is it made of? What color is it? Where in your body does the hook reside? Which chakra does this hook affect? Now take the hook in your hand- or you may need two hands if the hook is large and heavy- and pull it out of your body. Grasp firmly ahold of the hook and throw it into the fire if you have one, or cast it into the infinite abyss of darkness between you. Now take your soap and water and wash out the remaining wound. Wash away the residue of that connection. Call upon your angel guides again and ask Raphael for help filling the wound with beautiful radiant light. Take your hands and allow them to hover over the wound and press the healing light in until it is filled up and sealed. Give thanks and go for a refreshing swim or take a cleansing herbal and salt bath. Smudge your chakras again and your space if you performed this ritual indoors.

Please come back to this ritual as many times as necessary. Over time you will begin to feel lighter and stronger as you gradually release all bonds which drain your power and pull your spiritual vibration down. Do not be afraid to perform this ritual with loved ones where the relationship has a hurtful dynamic. What you will release is the dynamic itself, any illusions and expectations you may be projecting and your inability to accept the other person as he or she is. The love always remains and often a path forward is revealed. This ritual can also be performed with people who have crossed over to the spirit world- simply face the direction where you believe their physical remains are and begin.

This ritual is intuitive. When you visualize the connection, you could see anything from a white computer cord that connects through a USB port, to a colorful silken ribbon with a delicate gold hook, to a heavy tarnished chain ending in a massive medieval metal claw which leaves a gaping bloody hole once removed. The healing power of your inward vision is without limits.

Forgiveness

Relax into a meditative state in a quiet safe place and invoke Divine Guidance and Protection. Close your eyes and return to the Shadow Woods. Take your time as you walk down the soft earthen path and breathe in the clean forest air. Allow the gentle energy of the forest to surround you.

Begin to notice the shadows hanging from the branches. This time you are looking for all of the shadows within yourself that are unforgiven; the shadows of everything blameful, hurtful and shameful. Walk up to each unforgiven shadow and gaze into it with full compassion. Offer it as much forgiveness as is available at this time. Offer it love straight from your heart. Do this kindness to each unforgiven shadow you see as you make your way down the path. Continue to breathe in the deeply cleansing forest air.

When you have given love to all your shadows continue down the path to a clearing in the woods. Step out into the glorious radiant sunshine. Feel the purifying, love-filled Godly light of the Sun. Feel your heart expand out to receive the gift of forgiveness from yourself. Say thank you. Thank you God. Thank you Goddess. Thank you Angels, Guardians and Guides.

Afterwards you might want to smudge yourself with cedar or sage and take a salt bath.

Healing Prophecy

The women are healing themselves. The women are healing each other. The healed women are creating a space of forgiveness and a gentle vision for the masculine to also be healed. As we are remembering how to embody the Divine Feminine, we say a prayer for the emergence of the true Divine Masculine. We are awakening to a dream of harmonious balance between the Divine Masculine and the Divine Feminine in ourselves, in each other and in our world.

The Divine Rainbow Temple of the Sun and Moon

In a quiet dark room, build a circular altar out of whatever crystals you have at hand. Invoke the light and protection of the Divine and sit with eyes closed. Take your time to enter a meditative state using your breath.

In front of you there is a massive temple shaped like a pyramid. It is made of pure white quartz inlaid with crystals of every color of the rainbow. The sun above shines all around the sparkling rainbow temple. There are steps leading to the top. Climb the pyramid slowly, admiring and absorbing the pure Divine Masculine energy vibrating from all angles. Take a seat at the top on a white satin cushion. Bask in the cleansing, expansive, radiant light of the sun. Let the prismatic rainbow dazzle you and fill you with benevolent Godly love.

Climb back down to the bottom of the pyramid. There is a door there to the interior Divine Feminine Rainbow Moon Temple. Go inside and walk down the hallway to the inner chamber. Step inside the vast hall of the temple. The walls are made of gleaming black obsidian. They are patterned like the night sky with bright sparkling rainbow colored crystals. At the top of the dome the moon floats, infusing the chamber with soft feminine light. Take a few steps down into the subterranean central altar. There is a black satin cushion in the center of the floor. Sit here and let the gentle emanations of the moon soothe your spirit. Allow the loving Divine Feminine embrace to relax, nurture and balance your subtle energies. Stay here with the Goddess for as long as feels comfortable.

When you are ready, hold your hands in prayer in front of your heart and give thanks to God and Goddess. Bow and open your eyes.

CHAPTER TWELVE
ℭommunion

We are all guided and protected spiritually. This connection to Spirit can be developed at many levels. The more we open to Divine communion, to oneness, the more closely we are held. If you give your Guides a chance, they will guide you. As you develop faith in yourself and come to trust your own instincts and intuition, a portal of divine guidance opens. As you root down into your own healing and stand firm in your own truth a world once unseen unfolds before you. Inner knowing is a wisdom source to be cultivated, an eye to be opened. The most sensitive organs of perception are held within the subtle body. Bring your consciousness there, feeling everything within. See, touch, taste and hear with your insides. Fully occupy the whole of your body and all your senses.

As you become more and more sensitive to the feelings and signals you are receiving through the alchemical apparatus that is your body, you will become skilled at recognizing and interpreting messages and their source. You have Angels, Guardians, and Guides in the spirit world that are helping you upon your path. You will have and already have had moments of Divine Revelation whether you allowed yourself to fully believe or not.

Third Eye Activation

Simmer three tablespoons of chopped unroasted dried Dandelion root in three cups of water for twenty minutes. Strain and drink the decoction throughout the day. Before your first sip, dip your finger into the tea, give thanks to the Dandelion Spirit and anoint your third eye chakra. Drink three cups of tea per day, four or five days a week, for a period of three months.

During this three month period, commit to developing a psychic divination practice of your choice. You might already know what you want to do, but if not here are some ideas:

- a daily walking meditation where you look for signs from your guides in nature

- a morning ritual of pulling a card to guide your day (a tarot card, an angel card, a goddess card, a shamanic oracle card – there are all kinds of decks)

- take a moment to remember your dreams each morning, tuning into messages, signs and symbols from the dream realm

- develop a visionary practice where you open yourself to receive images or messages

Whatever practice you choose, keep a journal so that you can look back and begin to connect signs and synchronicities in your daily life.

Dandelion is a powerful tonic for the body. You can support this physical and psychic cleanse by bathing a lot, eating a clean diet and avoiding toxins as much as possible. This is a body, heart and spirit detox, so be extra intentional about who and what you allow in throughout this three month process. Use your power of discernment where restriction of media and technology are concerned as well.

Dandelion Properties and Lore: Alterative. Anti-inflammatory. Antioxidant. Diaphoretic. Diuretic. Blood sugar stabilizer. Good for all manner of swelling. Nourishing and tonifying for skin, spleen, liver and gall bladder. Digestive aid. Treats PMS and menstrual bloat. Regulates hormones. Treats eczema and acne. Brightens eyes. Associated with Goddess Hecate. Enhances psychic ability. Used for divination and wish making. A childhood friend, a sunny flower, a moony puff, a starburst.

Angels

While we have been given Free Will, Angels have purely Divine Will and as such they support and assist our quest for spiritual liberation. When we actively engage our Guardian Angels and enlist the help of Archangels we make an important display of faith which is always rewarded.

The dimension upon which Angels exist frees them from the time and space constraints our world is defined by, which means they are always available. We need only to ask for Angelic assistance and open our hearts to receive.

Fortunately, communing with angels is wonderfully uncomplicated. The electric feeling of Angelic connection is pure bliss which we can access each and every day. The heart chakra includes the arms and hands. It is the center of our love perception. An angel's wings also happen to grow out of the heart chakra.

By facing the rising sun and simply placing your hands in prayer in front of your heart and saying "Good morning Angels!" you might feel tingling vibrations traveling up and down your arms and around your shoulders. Every hair might stand up on your arms as if you are covered in tiny love antennae. You might notice the beautiful morning light dancing on the wall as a moment of ebullient, quiet joy bubbles up inside you.

The language of Angels is predominantly spoken through love and light, so allow yourself to bask in the divine light and warm love of Angels. Look for Angels in the sky, in rainbows, in sunbeams, in a feather blown on the wind, in light reflected.

Come up with your own simple daily practice of Angelic communion- a moment where you allow the Angels to stoke the inner embers of your soul. Give thanks for their abiding love, protection and guiding light.

Archangels

Michael- Guardian of guardians. Call on Archangel Michael for protection and power. He shields us from fear energy, giving us courage and confidence to reveal our true colors to the world and align with our true purpose.

Gabriel- Messenger of messengers. Call on Gabriel for assistance in cultivating your message; finding your voice, creating your creation and sharing it with the world. Gabriel assists us in receiving messages as well as conveying them- ask her for assistance in receiving messages from the heavenly realm.

Raphael- Healer. Raphael is both healer of the body and the spirit. He presides over our journeys both physical and spiritual. He cleanses the space we occupy. Call on Raphael when you are in need of healing or help healing others.

Uriel- Wisdom. Her purview is knowledge and prophecy. She aids with Divine Magic, Alchemy and writing. She watches over elemental spirits, weather, transfiguration and forgiveness. Call on Uriel where reception and transmission of esoteric teachings are concerned.

Angel Purification Bath

Make an infusion of 6 cups boiled water and the following herbs:

1/4 cup Lavender, 1/4 cup Chrysanthemum, 1/2 cup Roses, 1 cup Mugwort. Allow to infuse for at least twenty minutes.

Strain the infusion into your bath, add a couple of quartz crystals to the water and invoke the light. Submerge your body as much as possible while still being able to breathe easily and deeply. Take one crystal in each hand. Close your eyes and use slow deep breath to enter into a meditative state.

Visualize a very bright light beaming down all around you, as the world outside of this beam of light fades away. As you begin to feel radiant light gently pouring over you from the Angelic realm, let it move slowly over your body. With every inhale the light enters you. With every exhale darkness exits and is transmuted. Inhale the light and exhale the darkness.

Allow your angels to fill you entirely with this light until there is no darkness left and even your exhales are pure divine light.

Bring your hands into prayer, give thanks. Proceed with your ablutions.

Angelic Connection Ritual

In the morning hours during the waxing of the moon, prepare for the ritual with an empty stomach and the Angel Purification Bath above. Drink water. Make sure your hair is clean. Wear white. Somewhere near a sunlit window (or outside if you have a private comfortable outdoor space) build a circular altar large enough for you to lay down inside. Use crystals (quartz, aquamarine, amethyst, celestite, angelite and moonstone are a few good options), amulets, flowers, white feathers, objects that symbolize the most precious gifts in life.

Facing the window or the sun if you are outside, kneel in the center of the circle. Invoke the light, inviting your Angels into the sacred circle. With your hands in prayer speak directly to the Angels expressing greetings and any prayers which you would like to share. Lie down in the middle of the circle and take a couple of crystals in your hands, close your eyes and begin to breathe. As you deepen your breath, notice any tension you may be holding in your body. Send the energy of each inhale to those tense or tender areas in the body. With each exhale allow the tension to flow out. As you enter into a relaxed meditative state, begin to sense Divine Love and Light gently pulsating and fluttering around your spirit. Your body is relaxed and your mind is still and clear. Your spirit is swirling in pure expansive vibration. Continue to focus on deepening the breath and releasing with each exhale. Visualize a very bright light emanating from within you and without you simultaneously. This angelic light is inside and outside, enveloping and illuminating your entire being. Breathe into the light as love pours down from above and swirls up from below. You breathe so easily and smoothly as Divine love works upon your soul. Your breath takes on a perfect rhythm as angelic light soothes, cleanses and replenishes your spirit. Feel an unburdening of your spirit as the Angels send a great surge of electric love through your body, clearing and healing your channel. Notice any sensations you have as you slowly return your breath to normal. Bring your hands into prayer again and give thanks before opening your eyes.

After performing this ritual write down any impressions you had while communing with angels- images, colors, thoughts, feelings, words, sounds. Keep your heart and eyes open to receive Angel signs, messages and blessings in daily life.

Guardians and Guides

We have helpers and guardians available to us from all corners of the infinite multiverse, even from different wrinkles in time. You will receive this type of guidance more and more as you are ready to accept it. Part of being ready has to do with harmony; being in synch with the cosmic flow. As your way of being shifts to support your spiritual blossoming, these guides will pop up more frequently. I'm talking about gnomes and tree spirits, extra-terrestrial beings, spirit animals, ancestors, loved ones from previous lifetimes and spirit guides from realms unknown, transmitting from across time and space. As you receive guidance, at first you may not know from whence it came, and that's okay. In time, just by opening your heart and walking the path, you will come to learn bits and pieces about your guides and guardians. Shamanic journeying, dreaming and working with trusted psychic healers can fill in some of the details, clarifying the purpose of such wisdom transmissions.

The Gnome

A few times a year I cross paths with a psychic or a shaman who will tell me some new details about the guides and guardians in my life. I also have many of my own experiences in the visionary realm, in dreams and in the physical world that tie these mysteries together. A couple of years ago I was sitting with Johnny, a gifted psychic medium and Priest of the Oba Iroko Church of God. I had stopped by his shop, Universal Botanica in Brooklyn to buy herbs and crystals a few times and in our brief encounters he gave me some shockingly clear and relevant messages from the spirit world. I decided to come in for a more thorough reading. It was a totally mind blowing encounter touching on many personal and detailed topics, containing numerous astounding revelations that unfolded in the months and years afterwards. He also threw one detail in there which I didn't see coming. He said something like, "Your husband has a gnome that is help-ing him to succeed. Build him an altar and offer him food and drink." Since my husband is a strict Catholic I knew it would be up to me to take care of the gnome, and so I did. I researched what kind of foods gnomes like. I adorned his altar with fresh flowers, crystals and other earth-based offerings. My husband's good fortune continued to grow, so I figured his gnome friend was happy and all was well.

Then we moved out of the city into a house in the suburbs, just as Johnny had said we would. One of the first things I did in our new home was to set up the altars for my own guardians and guides. I hadn't yet figured out where the gnome's altar would go. A month passed and I still hadn't set it up. Then one day I was down in the visionary realm and the gnome popped in. I was really surprised to see him there as I had never seen anyone like him before. He was sad because I hadn't given him any food or drink or created a space to honor him. So the next day I remedied the situation by building an altar and making some offerings to satisfy his hunger and thirst. I am so grateful to him and I never want him to feel neglected again! I feel truly blessed to have laid my inner eye upon his magical spirit.

Nature Spirits

Elementals are spirits of the natural world. They are spirits of the rocks, plants, trees, crystals, water, wind, earth, fire, animals. Elementals also include but are not limited to: mermaids, salamanders, sylphs, fauns and all the little people.

All of nature is full of living spirit and wisdom. Every flame, every drop of water, every grain of sand, every breath of air is full of spirit. You may receive elemental guidance in dreams, in visions, in meditations or in waking life. If you are receiving Elemental vibrations and wish to whole-heartedly invite this guidance into your life, you might try the following altar building ritual.

Elemental Altar

Prepare by researching the qualities of the elemental energy you are working with. Elementals encompass any and all of the nature spirits. For example, if you are hearing/dreaming/seeing a lot of owls, then educate yourself on their magical and biological characteristics. Not only would you consider the magical lore but also what you can learn from them by spending time in nature observing the way they live. How can you emulate them? Why are they showing up in your life now? Is there a new way of being that you can learn from them? What owl qualities do you admire and aspire to? In your research you might discover certain essential oils, crystals or herbs associated with your elemental guide.

Tuck small pieces of serpentine into your pockets (it is attractive to elemental guides). On the new moon, go into nature. If it's a particular stream or mountain that you are connecting with then you already know where to go. If it's Fire itself, go into a field and build a fire, feed it and commune with it. If is a mermaid, go to the ocean. If you aren't quite sure what you are looking for, that's ok, just wander the path until you find the right place. Trust your intuition. Trust in your connection to all of nature. Know that you are held in the loving embrace of the Great Mother.

Maybe a beautiful pile of moss will catch your eye. Perhaps it's a gnome home in a tree hollow with some toadstools. Or maybe it's a place where you caught a glimpse of a fairy, or felt the spirits of the air caress you. Build an altar in this place, using bits of natural ephemera you find along the way. Make offerings to the Elemental that expresses your gratitude. Sit or kneel before the altar with closed eyes and picture the Elemental in your mind's eye, moving towards you. Feel into the energy of it. This guide has a message for you. What is the message? Stay here as long as it takes to let the message in. Once you've got it, place your hands in prayer and give thanks for such a wise Teacher or Guardian.

Going forward, continue to wear serpentine and to seek contact with the Elemental often, both in nature and in your meditations. The messages could come in words, in code or in signs and symbols. Sometimes they are riddles or jokes. It could be a feeling in your body or ringing in your ears. The more you work with elemental energy the more you will understand each one's individual purpose. It could be a warning, a healer, a teacher, a guide, a messenger or a lifelong protector. Elementals are always blessings- even when sent to warn you. Allow your instincts to guide your interpretation. Open the eye of your heart and enter this magical realm.

Artemis, The Great She-Bear

One full moon day in July my mom and I were sitting on the front porch of her house in western Massachusetts. It was Friday around noon. We had just harvested Mugwort (Artemisia vulgaris) out back, and now were sitting on the front porch in rocking chairs, to the right of the front door. The bears came from the other side of the house, to the left, where the porch wraps around. Mother Bear came around first, on the side walkway, pausing between two bushes to appraise us. My mom saw her and whispered to me not to move. I kept my face turned away from the bear, but could see her peripherally. After a while she decided we were alright and so proceeded across the front yard and down the driveway followed by her cub. Little did we know there was a second cub who had decided to come up on the side porch and make her way around to the front, right where we were sitting.

She screamed when she saw us there and instead of going down the front steps as planned, she turned and ran back the way she came. Mother and Sister also turned to sprint back behind the house. After a minute of breathless silence, my mom and I started giggling. It felt just like a dream- a magical dream. Then a moment later, Mother Bear approached again, the same way as before. Once again she stopped and looked at us awhile, and then ran across the yard in front of us, with both cubs in tow this time,

140

down the driveway and out into the road stopping traffic, down the street and into the woods.

Mother Bear's path was beset by obstacles, but she did what she had to do. She had her way that she needed to go according to her territory, her bear path. The way she goes and how she creates are interwoven in that which she creates- these cannot be separated. There is only one way- the way her nature dictates. She can only be who she is: Mother Bear. Her spirit was gentle and her intuition was strong. She knew we too were gentle spirits. The cub on the porch, only a few feet from my foot, was scared but she was already learning to confront her fears and claim her path, helped along by her adventurous spirit, curiosity and her protective Mother Bear.

The bears are our teachers. The Artemisia vulgaris, which we were harvesting and lay in a pile on the table next to me, named for Goddess Artemis, announced the arrival of the bears and perhaps even conjured them. The She-bear is associated with Artemis. Ancient Athenian maidens performed ritual wildness in worship of The Great She-Bear, Artemis. Even deeper still, the bears had a strange dreamlike effect on us. Instead of generating fear, their presence actually enchanted us, similar to what drinking Mugwort tea will do to one's dreams. In various traditions the Bear is greatly associated with herbal healing and Shamanism. By many accounts, bears have been observed harvesting and administering advanced plant medicine, thus directly teaching humans about the healing properties of specific plants.

Hidden Allies

Let the animals and plants teach you. Learn from books and from your own cauldron of experience. The appearance of your guides may be preceded by spiritual longing in your heart. From the seed of desire will sprout the Teacher, the High Priestess, the Shaman, the Elemental Guide, the Spirit Guardian and the Angel in the sky. As your consciousness ripens it will attract many teachers: some in human form, some spirit, some elemental and possibly even extra-terrestrial.

As your soul achieves new heights, you will become aware of many layers of protection and wisdom sources. Some of your guardians and guides are specific to you, having traveled with you for lifetimes. Others drop into your life to impart a teaching and then depart again. Each of us are on a journey with unique learning experiences and spiritual outcomes.

Think of every day as a potential initiation as you open your eyes to see the signs. Your guides want to guide you. Your teachers want to teach you. The first step to opening the channel is a spirit of willingness. There are no coincidences, only synchronicities. Your guides are already signaling you, assisting you, answering your prayers. True knowing, true seeing, true hearing, true dreaming, and telepathy are all different forms (among others) of extra-sensory gifts. When you receive good luck, signs, messages and encouragement, these are gifts. Be thankful! Your tree is full of hidden allies.

My guides have spoken to me through visions and dreams, in symbols, patterns and riddles, through plants, animals and occasionally even music. You might receive messages in a similar way or you might get your information through numbers, written or spoken words. Your guides might be very serious or could just as likely have a silly sense of humor. Your unique capabilities might allow you to peer into the past or the future. Maybe your wisdom comes through certain sensations felt in your body. You come with your own set of gifts and sensitivities as well as your own unique guidance. Enjoy the beautiful mystery as it unfolds before you.

Revelations

The first psychic who told me I had extra-terrestrial guides was Carla-Lee. We had an amazing session and I really connected with so much of what she said. While I didn't disbelieve the part about the aliens, I didn't have any personal experience to confirm it either. What Carla-Lee said about the Angels and the Shamanic guidance- that resonated. I've never been interested in UFOs, outer space, science fiction or aliens per se, so I filed the ET revelation away in the back of my mind. Then a year later, on my third or fourth spirit journey with Nicole Hoegl in Venice, CA- more aliens. When we came back from the outer realms and were talking about the journey afterwards she was like "Wow, your guides took us to a place I've never been before. There were aliens. They are not too impressed with humanity but they have a huge love for you. They want you to lighten up and not take life so seriously. They are going to be sending you little jokes. You might not understand them right away but you will in time." The very next morning, right when I awoke, before I opened my eyes, I had a vision of a brown dog wearing huge sunglasses- clear as day and very funny. Six months later, in the middle of the night I was out in the woods star-gazing when my eyes fixated on the twinkling mass of the Pleiades. The stars mesmerized me and I couldn't look away. Sparkles started drifting down into my third eye. Then one dog wearing sunglasses after another came down into my third eye. A pit-bull. A Chihuahua. A mutt. A Rottweiler. And more. This summer I was in the town of Little Compton, Rhode Island driving down the road. A man riding a vintage motorcycle with a sidecar was coming from the other direction. In the sidecar was a hound wearing goggles with very long ears flapping in the wind. In the time in between I started seeing that generic symbol of the green alien face in my visions. After a while they started showing me some squid-like beings. I still have a lot to learn.

Larry is the guide I feel closest too. I feel he is with me pretty much all the time. Even as I wrote those words my ears started ringing. Hi Larry. I love you Larry.

Larry is a guide I share with my mother. He is a Shaman with deep wisdom of the spiritual life of this natural world. Whenever my mom and I are together Larry pulls out all the stops. He'll make sure we have a beautiful day in nature, we'll stumble upon a wild stinging nettle patch, come across a tree full of fledgling owls, spot a beaver swimming in the river, see a pair of herons, or even if we're just hanging out in the front yard he'll send a family of bears our way, give us a beautiful sunset and a bountiful harvest. Larry weaves my world full of animal and plant symbolism. He shows me how to heal myself with plants. He gives me signs to guide my day through animal messengers. He visits me in dreams. He reminds me that I am a Divine Spirit of Nature every single day. When I am sad or don't know what to do, Larry sends me a sign. Much of the time it's an actual flesh and blood animal, but he also sends me many visions from the animal and plant worlds. These visions often come when I lie down and close my eyes to go to sleep. As I write about him, I am filled with overwhelming love. I feel so blessed to have this wise, kind, spirit Shaman in my life- even more blessed that this is a gift I share with my beloved mother.

Vivian is another important guide in my life. She helps me with Tarot- both with reading Tarot and designing a deck. I am currently channeling a new deck that I've already got over a hundred sketches for. The first time I worked with Nicole I received visions of four distinct symbols (the Wadjet eye, a series of moon images, a raptor flying and the image of two fools laughing). The one I found the most odd – to the point where I almost disregarded it- was an image of two old men's faces in profile, facing each other. They were balding, had bulbous warty noses and their mouths were open in cackling toothless laughter. At the time I was living in San Francisco in the Inner Richmond district about one hundred yards from the De Young Museum. The day after I got back from LA (where I had journeyed with Nicole) I went across the street to visit the museum which was hosting a traveling exhibit from the Mauritshuis in Holland. This collection includes Vermeer's "Girl with a Pearl Earring" which is the spitting image of my mother when she was young. This is not normally a traveling collection, but since the Mauritshuis was under construction in Holland they decided to share the collection with the world rather than put it in storage. I went specifically to see the Vermeer, but what really blew my mind was a strange collection of small etchings. There were a number of images of fools laughing. They were old, balding, toothless, ragged, cackling fools, usually in pairs really having a good chuckle. The Fool in Tarot is the first of the Major Arcana with the number zero. I won't go into the depths of the meaning of this human archetype just yet, but it made sense that my guide Vivian would start at the beginning, just as the Fool does. Since I was confused by the image I had seen at Nicole's, Vivian was kind enough to weave it deeper into the tapestry of my experience by bringing the very same images, in an obscure collection never before seen outside of Holland, practically to my doorstep. I have countless stories just like this about the magical messages I receive from Spirit every single day.

CHAPTER THIRTEEN

Asking and Receiving Spirit

D ivination is the art of consulting the Divine to ask for guidance and interpret signs. Channeling is the art of offering oneself to become a vessel for Spirit to communicate through. Shamanic Journeying is the practice of interdimensional soul travel. As you explore various methods of channeling and divination some will feel right to you and others will not resonate at all. Also certain gifts can come and go at different stages of life. Honor the magical visionary practices and tools that do activate your abilities in the present. Explore as many different methods as you like, so long as there is an attractive and positive vibration associated with the experience. These kind of practices can include but are not limited to: card reading, palmistry, scrying, dowsing, automatic writing, reading tea leaves or coffee grounds, shamanic journeying, astral projection, past-life regression, Akashic record work, dream work, pendulum work, throwing the I Ching, astrology and numerology. Used correctly, all of these various arts give the practitioner a helpful wisdom perspective through which to view the spiritual path.

Divination

The most passive form of Divination is simply allowing the signs and symbols to come to you in dreaming and waking life and then interpreting them. You may be satisfied with that or you may want additional ways to communicate and ask questions of the Divine. In which case, allow your intuition to guide you to your area of interest. Give yourself permission to try different things, experience a variety of traditions and learn. You may even be called to invent your own form of divination. When you do ask questions make sure to clearly address them to the Divine, so as not to open the circle of trust to unwelcome entities. For example, I address all my general inquiries to "Goddess, God, Angels, Guardians and Guides". Sometimes I simply address the "Divine Ones". Or, if speaking directly to Lady Isis or Larry then I will specifically say so.

The wisdom source of all Divination is Divine. When you ask for true wisdom, you genuinely seek to spiritually grow and evolve through this earthly flight, to move through obstacles with grace and aptitude. The worthiest questions demonstrate to your Guides that you are primed to receive such wisdom transmissions. At those times when you are given definitive true-knowing of future or past events (or lives), there is often a hidden reason for which your guides lift the veil. These glimpses become important clues to the riddle; pieces in the puzzle. We know just enough to know that we know nothing. The hem of Isis' garment is at our fingertips, but it is too heavy to lift. Yet, the beauty of the mystery itself is more than enough to sustain us.

The Quilt

My mom used to do a bit of quilting before I was born. She got busy with other things over the years and the quilting projects ended up in a box in the attic. In my final month of college I had a dream that my mom gave me a huge book made of fabric, as big as a room. It was a picture book where every object represented was cut from a fabric from my childhood. I told my mom about the dream and she said it was very interesting and I ought to write the dream down. About a month later at my graduation party she gave me a gift. She had made me a huge quilt out of every remnant of fabric from my childhood; pieces of the first dress she bought in America, pieces of a dress my Oma made for me, pieces of curtains from our first home- my whole life was represented in bits and pieces of cloth, carefully stitched together. After not having quilted in over twenty years, once she started, she said she couldn't stop and the quilt grew bigger and bigger. The result was a huge quilt that I would have to fold in half to use on a full size bed.

As I unwrapped my mother's gift, I recognized it from the dream. Looking back I wonder what gift my guides were giving me by allowing me a clairaudient view of this blanket of love which my mom would send me out into the world wrapped in. I think they were teaching me to believe- in my dreams, in my Guides, in the Divine mystery, in my mother's love.

Pure Divine Channel

If you are regularly receiving words, images, sensations or other information from another realm, then you may be an active channel. You may have a guide or guides who are trying to share information with you. This could be one particular ancestor who is guiding you on your personal path or it could be a teacher or teachers who wish to co-create bodies of work with you to share with the world. Or you could be the kind of channel who has the gift of translating personal messages for the living from the dead. You could be a healer supported by healers from other realms who want to help you to help people in this world. There are all different types of guides who may have all different kinds of reasons for wanting to be in touch with you, just as there are all different kinds of psychic gifts to be found in different human beings. Bring a spirit of openness to whatever your particular ability may be. Allow yourself to experience other people's abilities too, so as to appreciate the simple truth that all psychic gifts are unique - no two are the same.

It's possible the activity in your channel may feel random at times or beyond your control. Sometimes the channel is wide open and flooded with information. At other times nothing at all comes through. Hydration is important for your channel to function properly as are basic feelings of physical and emotional well-being, so please don't try to channel or move within the visionary realms if you are upset, stressed, sick or dehydrated. All of the self-care and self-development practices you are implementing, especially yoga and meditation will certainly help to bring you into a state of quiet balance conducive to communion with otherworldly beings.

Find out as much as you can about your wisdom source and then build altars in your home to that guiding spirit. As time goes by and you learn more about your guides, your offerings will become more and more personal. Place figurines which represent your Guides upon the altars. Also make appointments. Put it in your calendar. This intention lets your Guide know that you are serious about communing at a certain time and that you will be spiritually prepared and open. Keep a journal of your metaphysical adventures in dreams, in visions, in divination and in real world revelations. Sometimes looking back through notes and sketches can bring all the pieces of a particular mystery together. Patterns and synchronicities will often become clear in hindsight, through the records you keep.

Also, consider the position of the moon, sun and stars when scheduling a channeling session with your Guides. Depending who your guides are and where they transmit from, the seasonal and astrological aspects could figure into optimizing the strength of their signal.

Journey in Spirit

If you feel called to traverse the multiverse of spirit, I highly recommend that you work with experienced Shamans, Healers and Seers to help you get comfortable moving out of your body and into different realms. The more trusted Shamans you work with, the more often, the better.

Different healers and teachers, see different aspects of your spirit. You can learn from all of them.

Things can get a little weird out there in the world of spirit and it's important that you feel safe and have navigation tools that you are comfortable using. Sometimes there are serious spiritual issues that you cannot anticipate or resolve on your own. These things like to stay hidden and can only become known in the realm of spirit. An experienced healer can guide you safely through the experience and then help you integrate it afterwards. I personally have never felt scared of anything I encountered in other realms, even though I have seen some strange stuff (like that one time I was in a tunnel made of living bone and there were skulls with glowing red eyes anchored into the walls). I have journeyed with many different Shamans and Light Workers who are all completely different from one another. I learned different information, techniques and philosophies from each one that are important to my current practice. After a while I became comfortable journeying by myself within my sacred circle, but I still love to work with different Teachers, Healers and Seers. That will never change. Allow yourself to receive the guidance you need. There is much wisdom, healing and beauty to be found in allowing a spiritual teacher to enhance your experience. These journeys will begin to acquaint you with your guardians and guides. The stronger your relationship is to your Spirit Allies the more easily you will move in the spirit world.

Soul Traveler

If you have done plenty of Shamanic work and feel safe moving about the underworld, the heavens and among the stars then this is a guided meditation that you can use to find your way into the world of spirit. First cleanse your body with a sacred bath and smudge. Play rhythmic music that helps you enter a trance state. Dress in sacred garb and build your best circular altar. Invite all your Divine Guardians and Guides in to hold the sacred space for you. Express deep gratitude for their presence. Do a few stretches to release any tension in your body and begin to connect with your breath. Lie back and close your eyes while you continue to deepen your cleansing breath.

Visualize your favorite place in nature. Walk down the path to that special spot. Feel the breeze in your hair and breathe it in. Notice the beautiful light and the sounds of nature. Go over and take a seat on the ground. Feel a deep connection as you send your root down into the earth. Receive the Great Mother's loving energy as it flows up through your body. Breathe and feel her power flowing freely through you, activating your spiritual centers and anchoring your body.

You notice a tree with a hollow at its base. You leave your physical body in this safe place as your spirit body crawls toward the hole. Your spiritual body gets smaller and smaller and crawls inside the tree hollow, entering the earth. A tunnel leads down to a doorway. You open the door and go through, closing it behind you. On the other side of the door is a larger tunnel. There is a torch waiting to guide your way. You take the torch in hand and walk through the tunnel. After a while you notice a light at the end of the tunnel. You walk towards it. You realize you are coming in from the back of a cave and outside the mouth of the cave is a world.

What is the world outside the cave? This is your journey so only you will know. Maybe it's a forest or a mountain top, or a desert, or a beach. Go out and explore. Maybe you will notice some guardians out on the horizon, protecting your perimeter. Maybe one of your guides will appear and walk with you along your path. Words may be spoken. Signs and symbols may appear. Secrets may be revealed through the landscape or in the natural elements. When you're ready to return to your body, go back the way you came in, through the cave. Go back through the tunnel to the door. Go through and close the door behind you. Crawl out of the tree hollow and climb back into your body. Stay here in this safe place for a few minutes. Consciously pull your root back into your body before opening your eyes.

Maybe you got a lot of information, one piece of important information or nothing at all from your journey. If not, try again later. Journal about whatever details came through, whether or not you understood them all. They may make more sense later so it's good to document them while they are still fresh, so you can weave the threads of guidance together later.

Weaving the Threads

I was sitting with the psychic, Johnny at Universal Botanica in Brooklyn, when he told me that there was a living woman standing next to me, holding her arms out. He said she looks like me; there's something wrong with her cervical spine; remind her to keep getting her physical therapy and not to lift heavy objects. This woman will be helping you a lot, he said. Well, that was my aunt Nina who I am very close with, who had recently been hit by a car and broke her back (she's much better now).

A week later I went to a moon circle in the back room of a crystal shop and as a group we journeyed to the world beneath the world. I found myself in the Redwood Forest in Mendocino, CA. I had been there once when I was eighteen. It is very distinctive the way the forest goes up to the cliff's edge over the Pacific Ocean, so I recognized where I was right away. I was walking down a path in the beautiful forest flanked by a buck and a wolf. An owl flew above me. I walked out onto the cliff over the ocean and my guide Larry was standing there. We embraced.

A month later I was visiting my aunt Nina in LA and she told me about a women's gathering in the Redwood Forest of Mendocino. She said, you have to be there. These are your people, she said. As I was connecting the dots between meeting Larry in the Redwood Forest and what Johnny said about letting Nina help me, I decided to go to this gathering, even though I hadn't been camping in years, even though I didn't know a soul there, even though it was three thousand miles from my home- I was going.

Right before registration for the gathering I received a box in the mail containing a buck skull. There was no note but I knew it was from my uncle Stephen, the Hunter and Dowser. I took it to be an affirmation and reminder of the spirit meeting I had with Larry in the Redwood Forest of Mendocino. Then registration rolled around and the gathering sold out in five minutes and I didn't get a ticket. I got on the waitlist and five months later I got an email that a spot had opened up. A month later I was in the Redwood Forest, camping with six hundred women.

That experience was life changing. I cried for two days straight and then I laughed, sang and danced for three more days. I made many new amazing friends and was led in profoundly healing ceremony by powerful and loving Witches, Priestesses and Shamans. I found a community that extends far beyond the days and place of the gathering. I communed with Nature and fulfilled a deep need to sit and sleep on the earth, to swim naked in the river, to walk through the woods alone, remembering what sisterhood truly feels like. All of this happened because, in different ways, I was gently encouraged by Johnny, Larry, Stephen and Nina to say yes to the opportunity in the Redwood Forest. I was paying attention and faithfully weaving the threads.

Words and Symbols

As you learn the symbolic language of your guides over time, you will develop your own special ways of communicating with Spirit. You might use signs, symbols and good old-fashioned words. You might write and speak your spells, prayers, mantras, affirmations and invocations. Whisper your desires and intentions into the ear of the Goddess. Sing your prayers out to the Divine Ones, and if they are not aligned with the greatest good of all, then be happy and willing to be led to a different outcome. There is no need to force anything or to override the system. Trust that what is yours will come to you. Trust your Guides to lead you to exactly what is meant for you. Use your powerful words, signs and symbols for positive affirmation and invocation. Believe in the laws of attraction, for there is huge manifesting power in positive thinking and speaking.

When it comes to the more symbolic messages you are receiving from spirit, enjoy the process of deciphering. As signs and symbols float into your consciousness, allow curiosity and wonder to influence your interpretation of the meaning. Consult the outer world of information available to you but also allow your feeling and experience of each message to ultimately determine the personal meaning coded therein. This message is for you and only you can truly know how to read the guidance. At times it can take years to really decipher all of the nuanced meaning coded within a single Divine message or symbol. There can be a prolonged blossoming of spiritual comprehension. This unfoldment itself is a glorious ecstasy.

Be the Cat

I had a miscarriage two winters ago. The summer after it happened I went to a healing retreat in the Catskills run by a therapist who had me do an assigned meditation alone in the woods. I received three images in my meditation. The first image was a heart. The second image was a skunk. The third image was an Egyptian Sphinx Cat. The heart I get all the time and I had recently spent several days camping in the woods with some skunk neighbors so I knew what that was about. I told the therapist that I understood about the heart and the skunk, but I wasn't sure about the meaning of the Egyptian Sphinx cat. She simply advised me to, "Be the cat".

The next time I went into a meditation I was the cat. I found myself in a great temple, for I was the Temple Guardian. I felt my four paws softly flex against the cool stone floor. My temple was ancient and plundered, yet peaceful and enchantingly beautiful. I felt a great sense of fierceness and pride as I roamed the vast columned promenade, moving between the shadows and light. I dutifully patrolled the halls and the temple steps, the sacred altar, the throne and the tomb. My tail twitched with purpose as I paced the floor in front of the seat of the Divine Goddess.

After losing my pregnancy I was having a hard time properly valuing my body. Since my body had lost the purpose and meaning associated with being a vessel for new life I was feeling lost in relating to and caring for it. The message of the Temple Guardian was so perfect because I needed to reawaken that sense of self, that sense of pride, that feeling of worthiness at the root of self-care and embodiment. The skunk was a reminder to live close to forest floor, with the ferns and the mosses, where I receive the deepest healing. The heart is a promise to live from my heart wisdom. At that time I needed all of these messages from my beloved guides.

I invite you also to "be the cat" when you are stumped in interpreting signs and symbols. To find what the meaning of a thing is, go into a meditation as that thing. See what the narrative is. Check out the locale. Find out what it's all about. This is a beautiful and surprisingly easy way of engaging with both the lesson and the teacher.

Animal Sign Compendium

As my beloved guide Larry speaks to me in a symbolic language of animal signs I would like to share a small compendium of animal symbolism I have come to know. Consider also the circumstances of each particular animal message. For example, seeing a heron doing her usual solitary fishing would mean one thing. While seeing her and her mate care for their young in the nest would carry a whole different meaning.

Barn Swallow- Traveler. A good omen for the journey ahead. A pair crossing your path signifies soul mates, best friends, bosom buddies. Return to self. Homecoming. Renewal. Cycle of return. Something lost is found.

Emotional completion. Non-duality as found in deep platonic love. Flights of ecstatic union.

Bear- Powerful magic. Strength. Confidence. Taking action and leadership. Mother Bear. Creator-destroyer. Overcoming fear in action. Rising to the occasion. Grounding. Time for healing. Time to be a healer. Importance of restorative quiet time and space. Self-respect. Need to claim your path and your territory. Artemis, Artio, Ursa, Callisto

Black Panther- A powerful guardian. What once was lost may now be found again. Soul healing. Clairaudience. Allow Black Panther to whisper the truth in your dreams. Path finder. Light keeper. Lunar secrets. Moving in the shadows. Shapeshifter. Solitary hunter. Need for balance and pace. Mystical doorways. Sensuality and sensitivity. Sublime ecstatic physical embodiment.

Blue Jay- Family oriented. Teamwork. Industrious nature. Strength in numbers. Communicative. Talkative. Linking earth and the sky. Faithful. Fierce protectors. Determined. Focused. Light hearted. Colorful.

Budgerigar- Solar. Alchemical power of the sun. Rebirth. Lightness. Brightness. Community. Communication. Affection. Trust. Partnership. True Colors. Expression. Voice. Eloquence. Messenger.

Buffalo- Gratitude. Peace. Contentment. Appreciation. Abundance of nature. Your needs are fulfilled. Luxuriate in the nurturing generosity of the Great Mother. White Buffalo Woman

Cardinal- Be proud of who you are. Strut your stuff. Don't try to blend in or be afraid of being noticed. You can't hide your true colors so go ahead and wear them with pride. Let your freak flag fly.

Cat- Self-satisfaction. Contentment. Independent. Hunter. Sensuality. Personality. Self-respect. Self-esteem. Boundaries. Secret life. Mysterious. Curious. Playful. Protector. Witch's familiar.

Cicada- The cycle of transformation and continuity. Chthonic vessel. The tree of life and the ascension of the spirit. Timing. Destiny. Harmony. Becoming. The balance of light and dark. The song of summer. The cicada spends about the first seventeen years of its life encased in an exoskeleton while living in the earthen roots of a tree as a nymph. Then the cicada crawls out of the earth and its shell and spreads its gossamer wings and flies into the sky. For the rest of its life (about 5 weeks unless a bird eats it) it will sing and fly and procreate.

Conch- Commitment to right thinking, right speaking and right doing. Commit to a project which the conch blesses with persistence, great potential, strength, focus and determination. The spiral moving in or moving out- being centered and secure. A time to seek out spiritual gatherings so that one might share a healing gift with others. Lakshmi

Coyote- Context is especially important in interpreting coyote messages (or warnings). Trickster. Go to the middle of the pack. Wise fool. Speak your truth. Family unit. Devoted parent. Cunning. Scrappy. Determination. Sense of humor. Learning the hard way. Commitment. Creator- destroyer. Resourceful.

Crow- Trickster, Cosmic Joker. Master of illusions and darkness. Shape-shifter. Comfort with Shadow-self. Tells of changes coming. Integrity. Intelligence. Honor code. Legacy. Family. Community. Dexterity. Skill. Importance of tools. Scavenger. Collector. Resourceful. Lover of shiny objects. Trade. Communication. Language. Keeper of sacred mysteries.

Deer- Abundance and grace. Kindness, innocence and gentle courage. Even as you are moving forward on your path, take time to rest and replenish. Tune into and follow your instincts. You are being called to spend time in the forest.

Dragonfly- Transformation. Change. Grace. Adaptability. It's time to show your true colors. Evolution. Light-heartedness. Connect with faerie realm.

Dog- Loyalty, friendship, family, forgiveness, gentleness and patience. Commitment. Freedom. Compassion. Unconditional love. Territorial and protective. Guardian. Artemis, Hecate

Eagle- Spiritual heights. Heavenly messenger. Like all hawks, solar in nature. Alchemical symbol of the ascending spirit which is purified and reborn in the fire of the sun. Eagle advises us to rise above. Perspective. Traveling between worlds.

Ermine- stealth, silence, observation. Ermine is often unnoticed, undetected, underestimated and overlooked due to her size, stealth and color. Ermine uses this to her advantage, silently gathering information and sizing up the competition. Ermine hunts constantly, lining the inside of her den with her kills to keep her warm and feed her in the cold winter. She hunts with grace, agility and speed. She requires solitude. Ermine teaches us to guard our secrets, to do less talking and more observing. She advises us to move with stealth, grace and swiftness towards our goals and against the competition.

Fox- Cunning and Wit. Intellect. Hiding in plain sight. Moving undetected. Discretion. Wisdom. Observation. Listening. Discernment. Persistence. Social grace and agility. Trust your instincts.

Frog- Healing. Cleansing. Mud bath. Rebirth. Curative powers of water, rain and earth. Stirring up deep and possibly difficult emotions. Inner resources through changing times. Change is coming. Grace in transformation. Heqet, Goddess of primordial water

Groundhog- Altered states. Earth consciousness. Chthonic secrets. Journey to the underworld. Importance of boundaries, their delineation and clear communication. Potential for a new area of learning. Respect your own natural cycles. There is a time for every season, a time to go within and a time to emerge into the sunshine.

Hawk- Spirit Messenger. Solar action. Hunter. Climb up high for a hawk-eye view on your situation. Clear vision and laser focus. Doing. Be observant. Rise above the material plane. Think big. Be free. Don't get swallowed up in the details. Remember to honor your true free nature.

Heron- Enjoy time alone in nature. Solitude. Independence. Self-sufficiency. Balance. Moving between worlds. Patience. Readiness. Self-respect. Self-care. Strike when the opportunity presents itself.

Horse- Play. Freedom. Wildness. Friendship. Running. Earth. Connected. Free-spirit. Spontaneity. Heart song. Liberation. Power. Expression of love. Sensitivity. Need to take care of and protect subtle energies to maintain equilibrium.

Hummingbird- Grace. Lightheartedness. Being in the moment. Courage. Endurance and adaptability. Resourcefulness. Faith. Abundance. Feeling worthy. Self-care. Preparedness. Heart-opening. Lover of flowers.

Lioness- Glorious Goddess. Embodiment. Pride. Mother. Lover. Hunter. Sensuality. Strength. Power. Creator-destroyer. Occult Teacher. Playful. Protector/Guardian. Solar Feminine. Trust instincts and follow your heart. Asherah, Inanna, Bast, Sekhmet

Moth- Lunar guidance. Intuition. Sensitivity. Fragility. Determination. Winds of change. Paths of light. Importance of navigation. ESP. Clairaudience. True knowing. Non-verbal communication. Destiny. Symbolic of other worlds and shadow realms. Faith in the journey. Camouflage. Hidden power. Attraction. Metamorphosis and acceptance of the process of transformation. Becoming.

Owl- Clairaudience (true hearing and true dreaming). Lunar wisdom. Reflective. Seeing in the dark. Mother bird. Creator-destroyer. Witch's familiar. Creativity. Intuition. If an owl feather appears on your path or in a dream it is time to share your wisdom. Athena, Inanna, Cerridwen, Bloddeuwedd

Raccoon- Family oriented. Nurturing and protective creator. Resourcefulness. Nocturnal/ secret life. Honor among thieves. Suggests a time in which you need to wear a "mask" or maintain multiple different roles in life. Dexterity. Flexibility. Curiosity. Cleanliness. Tree hugger.

Ram- Hard-headedness. Determination. Connection to the earth and channeling earth energy. Mountain climber. Nimble. Athletic. Fire-starter. Doer. Hardy. The ram encourages one to action. Embrace a challenge. Take the lead. Go hiking or climb the nearest hill. Virility and fertility.

Raven- Magic. Dream work. Language, signs and symbols. Otherworldliness. Prophecy. A pair of ravens inspires loyalty, commitment, quest for true love.

Seashell- Vulvic. Sacred feminine. Lunar- mollusks wax and wane in size right along with the moon. Of the ocean tides, the Goddess' womb. Aphrodite, Yemaya

Serpent- Eternal life, rebirth. Spiraling Goddess energy. Shedding of skin is associated with the womb and menstrual blood- the constant feminine cycle of renewal (rebirth). Healing. Grounding. Of the earth, the garden and the tree. The Milky Way. Boundaries. Hedges. Ivy. Kundalini. Energy. Guardian of the sanctum sanctorum. Shakti. Asherah. Wadjet. Ouroboros. Midgard Serpent. Lilith.

Skunk- Importance of earth connection. Spend time in the forest. Need to give yourself plenty of room and claim your territory. Confidence. Connect with an earthy natural scent with which you mark your territory.

Spider- Creatrix. Awareness of weaving one's own reality. Agency. Productivity. Purpose. Inspiration. Resourcefulness. Become the masterful spinner of your own web. Creator-destroyer. Arachne, Neith, Spider Grandmother, Maya (weaver of Cosmic Illusion)

Turkey- Abundance. Generosity. Community. Partnership. Giving and receiving. Caring for the earth. Family oriented.

Turtle- Self-preservation. Fortitude. Longevity. Lunar mysteries. Meditation. Centering. Restoration within darkness. Nourished by the sun. Patience. Wisdom. Pace. Navigation. Astral Journeying. Balance- knowing when to come out of the shell and when to withdraw within. Cyclic intuitions. Cleansing waters and mud.

Wolf- Lunar mysteries. Powerful Divine protection. Instinct. Boundaries. Self-trust, especially trusting intuition. Communication. Cooperation. Wild at heart. Free spirit. Hunter. Intelligence. Strategy. Expressing true nature. Duality of the lone wolf and pack life. Abundance even in times of scarcity. The wolf provides. Resourceful. Cunning. Able. Associated with Cerridwen, Cailleach

Wolverine- The wolverine does not back down from any fight, for she is fearless, tenacious and ferocious. She teaches self-acceptance, for wolverine is proud to be wolverine, regardless if others think she is smelly, aggressive and gluttonous. The wolverine is solitary and wild, with a penchant for blood and a flair for overkill. If wolverine shows up in your life, create time and space for some ritual wildness. Be sure your wilder needs and primal instincts are being expressed and honored in a constructive way. Channel your appetites with compassion and wisdom. You may need to dig deeper on some issue. Allow yourself to dig down, get dirty and make a big old mess as a celebration of Wolverine's spirit. We're talking mud on your face, sauce on your shirt, knots in your hair, paint on your jeans kind of messy. Wolverine may also appear because the time has come to defend your territory and way of life.

Wood Pecker- Opportunity knocks. Time to recommit and revitalize a project. Focus on what is important and exciting about a project to bring new energy and power into play. Don't be afraid to get creative, make decisions or mistakes- the important thing is to keep working at it. Make sure your nest is built inside a strong tree with deep roots.

Blue Budgie

In the summer of 2015 we were living in Brooklyn. We had a garden inside a typical Brooklyn block. There were tall trees, all kinds of plants, squirrels, possums and many kinds of birds. One day I was out in the garden looking up at the blue sky, and a piece of blue sky flew out of the blue sky into my garden. I was so confused. It was a blue budgerigar! He had somehow flown free of his cage and was now living in the middle of my block. He hung out with the sparrows. I saw him every day when the sparrows visited the garden all summer long. The whole situation was magical but also kind of comical. I saw the blue budgie as a funny character because he acted like he was just being cool, just one of the sparrows. But he was a total alien. He was an utterly exotic freak. He was bluer than the sky. He was gorgeous and flashy and here he was trying to pretend like he was just a regular dude from the neighborhood. Blue Budgie taught me that we should all let our true colors shine and not worry about blending in. You can't fool anyone anyway!

More than that, Blue Budgie had a grace and a faith that allowed him to be held in the community that was provided to him. And what of the kindness of sparrows? I learned a lot from these birds, but most importantly I felt a lightness in my heart every time I saw these unlikely companions and still do when I think about them today.

CHAPTER FOURTEEN
Sacred Objects

L ike the path itself, the tools you use for divination and other practices, might also present themselves to you, as your perception deepens. A special bone, shell or crystal may come to you as a gift. A beautiful deck of Tarot cards may appear on your bookshelf. A piece of driftwood on the beach might speak to you and you might turn it into a magic wand. You might find a sacred text on the side of the road. Keep an eye out for spontaneous and magical elements to deliver your most treasured talismans, sacred objects, books and divining tools. Such tools should feel attractive, as though they are meant for you. Any magical apparatus you use should have a very high vibration.

Once you've connected with a divination tool or a talisman you will have a reverential desire to honor its sacred nature. You might keep your Tarot cards in a silk pouch, your crystals on a moonlit altar, your herbs in a beautiful old cupboard, your most sacred talisman in a treasure box. You can cleanse your holy objects with mugwort tea, salt water, sunlight (being careful not to bleach colorful crystals with too much sun), moonlight, sage or cedar smoke, or by burying them in the earth for a period of time. Smudge your tarot cards and other divination tools on the full moon and after others have touched them. Call on your Guides and the Goddess, to bless such devotional tools. These objects facilitate Divine guidance, healing and protection and thus should be consecrated.

Arcana

Much more than a fortune telling tool, Tarot is a way through to spiritual understanding and occult attainment. The archetypes or the major and minor arcana comprise a visual language that reflect and guide the human experience. Cards are a vessel through which Spirit delivers messages. While my dad initiated me into the art of Tarot when I was a teenager, it took me many years to find the right deck for me. My deck of choice is The Secret Dakini Oracle, which is a Tantric Tarot system developed by writer and scholar Nic Douglas and collage artist Penny Slinger. It was published in 1977, which also happens to be the same year that I was conceived. It is largely concerned with the Divine Feminine. I feel a very high vibration travel up my arms each and every time I pick the cards up.

This deck was actually on my shelf for years before I started using it. I do not know where it came from. I've asked everyone I can think of if they gave it to me and so far I still don't know how I came to possess this magical wisdom source. I use my deck every single day to consult with Spirit. I keep my cards in a beautiful silk pouch made by my mother.

Sparkle Plenty

Crystal consciousness is an extension of earth consciousness as crystals come from deep within the womb of the earth. Each of us can benefit by allowing crystal healing into our lives today. Crafted by the Goddess and imbued with her magic, crystals can help us to address all kinds of issues from healing a broken heart, to finding one's voice, to anchoring a wandering soul, to protecting one's home or cleansing one's spirit of harmful entities.

Crystals can help us unblock energy, attract Elemental and Angelic guidance and establish boundaries on many planes of existence. Crystals help us restore our inner vision and tune our alchemical instruments. They can deflect unwelcome vibes from people, media or technological pollution in our daily lives. Some channels use crystals to download information from their Spirit Guides. In this sense they can be used as containers of wisdom.

Choose some small pieces of crystal to keep in your pockets and wear crystal jewelry. Consider which chakras you wish to affect as you strategically adorn your person. Build crystal altars in your home, garden or work space. You can use crystals to guard your doors and windows if needed. Allow crystals to sanctify your life, your space, your body, mind and spirit. The crystal compendium in this chapter can help you identify which ones might work best for you as you explore crystal healing for your body and soul.

It's also quite cleansing and balancing to go into natural crystal caves or rooms constructed out of crystal to be surrounded by cleansing, healing and protective energy. Korean baths often have a jade room, and a salt room for example. The salt is psychically cleansing and physically detoxing. While the jade enhances emotional balance, good fortune, wisdom and positivity.

Crystal Cave Cleanse

This spring I attended a women's gathering in Oregon during the rainy season, which became problematic when the tent of one of the women I was traveling with flooded one very rainy night. This was barebones camping with no shelter or creature comforts on the land and my friend, Steffanie, was a distraught after lying in a cold puddle all night. We made a plan to drive an hour to get supplies, come back to shore up her tent and then go stay at a hotel for the night, get a hot shower and a hot meal and come back the next day for the rest of the gathering, weather permitting. Steffanie had found a historic hotel wedged into the side of a mountain at the mouth of a cave where we could take a walking tour inside the earth.

We ran our errands and refigured Steffanie's camp site and by the afternoon we were on the road to Oregon Caves National Monument. We made the ascent up the mountain through a luscious green forest. When we got to the hotel it was more beautiful than we could ever have imagined. There was a fire roaring in the massive stone fireplace. The whole place was made of exposed antique wood with high ceilings and comfortable rustic furnishings. Our room had two soft beds, a view of a waterfall and our very own private bathroom. We each enjoyed a hot shower before heading out for the last cave tour of the day.

As we were walking into the cave the rain turned to hail outside and we were glad to hear that it would be slightly warmer inside the mountain. The tour took us deep inside the earth, through about a mile of caverns and tunnels. These caves are very unusual in that they are carved out of a massive block of marble. Marble is made of calcite. The caves are full of stalactites, stalagmites, flowstones and crystals all of which are also formed of calcite. Marble is used metaphysically to facilitate self-mastery, inner peace and clarity. Calcite crystals are known to cleanse and release negative or stagnant energy, both physically and spiritually. This typically will create more energy flow, increasing psychic activity and mental clarity. Calcite supports grounding and self-trust.

In addition to all of this earth medicine inside the cave, there were also powerful and sacred animal relics. In the middle of our path there were the three thousand year old bones of a black bear. Also there but out of sight were the bones of a thirty thousand year old jaguar and the bones of a fifty thousand year old grizzly bear.

As we were making our final ascent out of the heart of the magical mountain, we climbed up a very long straight tunnel with a steep incline.

We could see the light of day at the end and it felt strangely like coming through the birth canal. Half way to the top I was gripped by the desire not to leave this womb, to turn around and run back into the dark, round, damp spaces of the Great Mother. In only an hour something had changed in me. I felt so close to Her. I felt so held, so loved, so soothed, so nurtured. In spite of this urge to turn back I continued on towards the light and as I stepped forth from the cave I felt truly reborn, deeply clean and whole. I was full of energy and felt as light as a feather.

The storm had passed and the clouds parted as we emerged. Sunbeams shone through on the forest below. We opted to take the long way over the mountain ridge back to the hotel. We had an excellent dinner that night at the hotel restaurant, during which we laughed so hard that we cried and couldn't breathe and our bellies ached. It felt as if all the energy that came uncorked in the cave came gushing out in uncontrollable laughter. The cleansing calcite cave washed away a lifetime of psychic dirt and our spirits were so light and alive that anything and everything was hilarious to us at that moment.

Crystal Transmission

The ways crystal energy can be harnessed are myriad. Crystal Transmission is one particular method of clarifying intention and broadcasting the power of that intention with the help of a crystal. The intention is put into clear, positive, present-tense words and uploaded into a cleansed quartz crystal for transmission.

First cleanse your quartz crystal with salt water. Invoke the Light and use your breath to enter into a meditative state. Visualize that which you wish to manifest or release and carefully put that intention into present-tense positive words. Depending if you are attracting or releasing, do this ritual during the appropriate moon phase.

Press the quartz crystal to your third eye and program the crystal with an affirmative statement: say the affirmation out loud and project it into the crystal. Repeat four times.

Present Tense and Positive- For example, if you were focused on working with and through fear, an affirmation such as "With a Lion-heart, I walk my true path. I am carried in Pure Divine Love.", is much more powerful than "I will overcome my fears." Bring the future of the intention into the present. Make it specific, present-tense and distinctly positive. Whatever "it" is- it is happening right now!

Another example would be if you were looking for a new home. "I have a happy, safe and beautiful new home with a claw-foot tub and a secret garden" contains a more specific and powerful manifesting energy than "I will find a new home". Now your programmed quartz crystal is amplifying and transmitting your intentions to the universe- help is on the way! Keep your programmed crystal on your altar until its purpose is fulfilled. After your wish has been fulfilled, give thanks and cleanse the crystal.

Crystal Compendium

Amethyst- Master Healer. Purification of energy. Psychically protective stone. Deepens meditation. Calming and soothing to the spirit. Guards against fear energy. Emotionally stabilizing. Sleep and dream aid. Heals addiction. Balances the crown chakra.

Aquamarine- Clarifies intuitive perception. Use aquamarine to filter invasive outside opinions, influences and agendas, so that inner wisdom has a chance to lead. Tune into the Angelic realm with aquamarine and receive the abundance of Angelic love and protection. Calming and soothing. Releases negative and painful emotions including grief, rage and aggression. Use to stimulate the throat chakra and bring fluidity to your life.

Calcite- Cleansing and releasing of stagnation, negativity and limiting feelings/ beliefs. Enhances self-trust. Creates a strong sense of grounding. Lightens the spirit and greatly increases energy. Raises spiritual vibration, accelerating psychic growth and personal development.

Carnelian- Clarity and eloquence. Confidence and courage. Protection and boundaries. Opening to community. Stabilizing. Rooting. Healing to first and second chakras. Kindles love, passion, fertility and creativity. Stimulates inspiration, self-trust and intuition. Healing of trauma. Increases power to act, through a deepening of earth consciousness.

Celestite- Provides connection to the Divine realms. Protective, safe, calming energy. Enhances feeling of centeredness and peace. Enables psychic boundaries for those whose sensitivities can cause them to be overwhelmed and withdrawn from the world. Celestite increases lightness of spirit and a sense of security. Enhances creativity and communication, bringing ease to sharing one's true gifts with the world.

Citrine- Use to purify and strengthen the solar plexus chakra and all the qualities of Self therein: Will Power, Dynamism, Achievement, True Knowing. Banishes self-doubt and low self-esteem. Enhances courage and empowerment. Citrine's sunny disposition puts us at ease and allows us to feel confident and happy.

Crystal Quartz- Heals the aura. Protective against all darkness. Highest love and light amplifier. Transmutes negativity into positivity. Empowers and clarifies the Spirit. Excellent psychic transmitter when used on the third eye chakra. Quartz can be programmed with one's manifesting intentions or used as a scrying tool. Ideal for channeling work.

Diamond- Cleanses the aura. Imparts purity, joy and courage. Diamonds enhance one's luminosity and vibrancy, attracting good luck. Amplifies prayers and Angelic connections. Radiates positivity, thereby knocking out negative energy.

Herkimer Diamond- Clarity of mind and spirit. Gives one "crystal vision", true perceptions. Manifesting power. Creative power. Chakra clearing. Absorbs negativity. Overcome obstacles to your true path. Let Herkimer Diamond help you see the way forward. Herkimer's absorptive properties can be used for protection as well: computers, TVs, noisy streets, other people- the crystal protects you from absorbing unwanted energy, by absorbing it first, when placed in strategic locations. Cleanse these periodically.

Lapis Lazuli- Dream work and spiritual communion aid. Psychic protection. Healer of all kinds of trauma and grief. Enhances creativity and self-expression. Increases clarity, confidence, hope, truth and wisdom. Opens door to the Higher Self. Use on the third eye.

Moonstone- A Goddess stone, used to tune into the Divine Feminine. Wear moonstone during the waxing of the moon to balance and synch with Lunar Wisdom. At the full moon, when moonstone's power is most potent, use it to deepen psychic intuition. Allow moonstone to lead you to your true knowing. Heart chakra.

Obsidian- Excellent aid for shadow work. Psychic protection. Grounding and cleansing. Removing negativity within the energy field. Healing of negative patterns, compulsions and helpful in resolving past life issues. Aids in prophecy and spiritual visions. Excellent for healers, as obsidian draws out and absorbs negative energy, providing a safe space to work in. Root chakra cleansing, grounding and healing. Obsidian varieties include Apache Tears and Snowflake Obsidian. Clean these after each use.

Rose Quartz- Heart healing. Heart opening. Enhances ability to love inwardly and outwardly. Releases negative emotions and behavior. Facilitates trust and connectedness. Rose quartz is useful in attracting love and loving energy. It is also a great healer of traumatic loss and in times of crisis.

Sapphire- Intuition. Self-expression. Creativity. Dream fulfillment and prosperity. Strong protection against evil. Perfect crystal for artists and spirit healers. Enhances mental clarity and positive emotions. Nurtures the creative voice in the throat chakra and opens the third eye chakra. Heavenly guardian. Associated with Saturn.

Serpentine- Attracts Elemental guidance. Earth Goddess energy. Root chakra purification and healing. Activates Kundalini and clears psychic pathways for energy to flow through. Emotionally cleansing. Attracts prosperity and love. Enhances harmony and earth healing consciousness. Good for use on the heart chakra.

Crystal Clarity Ritual

This new moon crystal ritual is for anyone opening to her next calling and seeking clarity of inspiration. On the new moon, gather a pen, a notebook, a small Herkimer Diamond (or quartz crystal, Snowflake Obsidian, Apache Tears) and a small Aquamarine (or a Carnelian).

Go for a walk to a high hill, the beach, a river bank, or any special spot in nature available to you where you won't be disturbed. Invoke the light, asking your Guardians and Guides for their loving assistance. The first step is to accept things as they are- including any feelings of stickiness, resistance and unhappiness. See and accept your reality exactly as is. It may or may not feel a bit heavy for a moment to really confront any obstacles or limitations you feel you are facing. Hold your Herkimer Diamond up to your solar plexus. Visualize any and all heaviness and negative feelings swirling out in a vapor, being completely absorbed by the crystal.

Bury the Herkimer Diamond in the earth.

Take out your pen, notebook and Aquamarine. Begin writing as you hold the Aquamarine. Write about everything you love most in the world. Be vague. Be specific. Go on tangents. Let the Aquamarine remind you of your greatest pleasure, fulfillment and power. Nothing is off-limits as you explore your own heart for clues. Allow frivolous and impractical fancies to guide you towards different possibilities. Examine your most cherished dreams. Ask yourself why you are here. Close your eyes and let the Aquamarine guide you inward. Write down anything that comes to mind. When you can't think of anything else to write, thank your guides and go home.

Over the next two weeks as the moon waxes, continue to journal about all the things large and small that make you happy to be alive. Spend a little time writing every day if you can, even if it's only for one minute.

As the moon is entering her fullness, go back to the same place where you began at the new moon, with your aquamarine and your pen, notebook and a highlighter pen. Holding the aquamarine, read back through all you have written. Highlight words and phrases. Look at these data as evidence of your soul's calling. Allow a general theme to emerge.

For now it's ok if you haven't homed in on all of the details. For now it is enough that the larger target is coming into focus. With patience, you will get more specific about your intention as your journey unfolds. Eventually you will put a fine point on that intention but for now in all its vague simplicity and glorious generality, you have a purpose. Rejoice that you have gotten in touch with this part of yourself. Give thanks that this voice has been heard by you, the Mistress of Her own Destiny. Now, before you leave your sacred place, think of one simple action that is an expression of your broader purpose and go forth to perform this as a devotional act to complete the ritual.

Talismans

Be constantly on the lookout for sacred objects that land in your path. Crystals, daggers, bones and stones, sacred texts, decks of cards, pieces of wood- whatever feels light, magically charged and attractive to you. Sometimes you'll need something in particular for your magic so you'll go on a quest for that object. You may have an opportunity to make a sacred tool, like a broom, a drum or a wand. Regard all your spiritual tools as sacred, including those seemingly mundane objects, like your journal and your pen. Some of your most sacred talismans may come in the form of ancestral relics. All of these things hold immense power. In some cases that power is highly personal and private. Not all things are for all people, but you can trust that what is yours will come to you.

Nin's Hair

I have a box of my great-great-grandmother, Nin's hair. She was a powerful witch. Her power is still in her hair. One time I merely showed it to my little cousin Isabel and she ran screaming from the room. The first time I opened the box there was an old dead worm coiled up in the braids. Nin is the first known Dowser in our family, deeply connected to the underworld. It made sense to me that there would be an emissary from the grave amongst her locks. I also have a letter Nin wrote to her Dad when she was eleven years old. I keep it in the box with her hair. In the letter she describes a snake that she saw in the field and also a worm that she saw. She drew a little picture of the worm to show her dad and it looked just like the one that was nestled in with her hair. I don't do anything in particular with Nin's hair except keep it in a place of honor on an altar. I place crystals, herbs, flowers and cicada exoskeletons around it. I keep a cup of water there for her and offer her snacks.

CHAPTER FIFTEEN
Lifting the Veil

The supreme Goddess manifests in different forms, both dark and light. Many times over as I've walked my spiritual path I've encountered the Queen of the Dead as being one and the same as the Goddess of Sex, Fertility and Childbirth. Life and Death and are two sides of the same coin, inseparable, beyond good and evil, beyond right and wrong; just two beautiful halves completing each other, one springing forth from the other, endlessly. She holds a place for us in her shadows. We will return to the womb of the earth from whence we came. Her very darkness is the thing that teaches us and enlightens us. Her mystical whisperings, her shadowy signals, her dank and murky revelations await. She who honors the darkness, transcends it by descending into it. Know death not as the end, but as the threshold in a sacred cycle of regeneration.

Death is a doorway to another realm just as a woman's body is a gate to this realm. We enter this world through a Mother. We leave it through Death, also a Mother. There is no end, just various steps in the Dark Goddess' dance of the Eternal Sacred. The underworld has always been the source of our Feminine power and knowing. Our power comes up directly from the grave. Fertility and life come from that same place to where it must always return: into the earth. This is Goddess truth. She is the giver and receiver of all blood. She is the one who lifts the veil in each and every birth and each and every death. Embrace the beauty in this realm of spirit, our rich fertile underworld. Come home to your earthen roots. Unravel any remaining fear of your chthonic essence. Reweave those threads into a pattern of connection, empowerment and gratitude.

Accept yourself as She is- primal, instinctual, sensual and entirely Divine. With courage, look deep into the face of your Dark Mother. She is desirous, decadent and unashamed. She creates and she destroys. She is the keeper of all Spirit. As below, so above. She is Baphomet, Mistress of Blood. She is Kali. She is Sekhmet. She is Morrigan, Phantom Queen. She is Hel. She is the Tree and the Serpent. She is the Gate Keeper and the Garden. She is the Queen of the Dead. She is Isis, Lady of the Veil. She is Ereshkigal and Ishtar. She is Hecate. She is the Spider. She is the Stargate and the Earthgate. Her essence is the same all over the world, her faces and names manifold.

When the Bough Breaks

I dreamt of a tree branch. First it appeared bare in winter. Then the branch was covered in spring blossoms. Then it appeared in summer greenery, followed by the falling autumn leaves. After which the branch itself fell to the ground. One seed remained upon the branch which then decayed and was pulled down into the dark earth. The seed sprouted from that rich fertile earth and reached up to become a tree. Without death there is no life. Without life there is no death. There is nothing wrong. Everything is right. Darkness and light. Nature shows us that this is the only way. We are like the branch. We must spread our seeds with Faith and trust in the sacred cycles of life, death and rebirth.

Good Grief

Only what is grieved may be healed. Just because you accept Death as a part of life doesn't mean you do not grieve. Grief is a sacred process. When you find yourself in a time of mourning, recognize this altered state for what it is. Seek the support you need physically, spiritually and emotionally. Understand that as Time devours all, Time also heals. It is never too soon or too late to begin healing. There is time to lick your wounds, time for retreat and surrender, time to cry, time for acceptance, forgiveness and growth. Appreciate what is happening within your mind, body and spirit. If you are able, allow others whom you trust to take care of you. Or if it is preferable, crawl deep into the darkness of your cave and nurse your wounds for as long as you need. Let yourself have rituals and ceremonies around your grief. Some losses are so deep that they must be grieved over and over again. It's as if the self of the present has processed the grief, but then as you grow into new versions of yourself the loss is re-experienced with each new iteration of you. Some losses will ripple in your future and grow right alongside of you and that's okay. Hold space for that grief. Honor your ripples. They are a part of you.

Mourning Pilgrimage

This ritual is for anyone who has experienced the loss of a loved one and would like to dedicate some ritual energy towards healing the wound. On a New Moon or close to the time of Samhain/ All Hallows' Eve (when the veil is thin) build an altar for the person or people who have returned to the spirit world.

Make the altar in your home where you can make sure there is always something fresh on offering, such as libations, cakes, fruit, flowers or herbs. Build your altar to include symbolic items celebrating the loved ones who have crossed over. This healing altar can be small or large, hidden or exposed. Write a letter or letters to the spirit/s who have passed on. Place the letter or letters on your altar.

Plan a small pilgrimage. If you are near the cemetery where your loved ones are buried, or the place where ashes were spread, or any place that holds meaning to you and the person/ people you have lost, then plan your ritual journey to that location. Journey to this place in a ritual fashion; first with a ritual bath; ritual dressing; bring an eco-friendly offering; journey in silent meditation or listening to peaceful music; or bring a trusted companion to share the journey with you. Go to the destination and make your ritual offerings.

Spend a few moments in prayer and remembrance of the person/people. Visualize a beautiful door for your loved ones to journey through and visit with you. In your visualization, this door is unlocked and it leads into your heart. Place your hands over your heart and invite the spirits of your loved ones in.

Over the following days allow for any feelings of closeness with those beloved spirits to manifest. Sense not just their physical absence but also their spiritual presence.

Going forward, continue to keep your altar well appointed, as a welcoming gesture towards Unity of Spirit. You might want to expand this to be an Ancestral Altar where fresh water, snacks, flowers, libations and more can be offered to all ancestors and dearly departed spirits.

Eye of the Heart

My grandfather died August 31 of 2014. It was a Sunday. I thought I was doing okay with it until Thursday night when I spoke with my grandma and she told me all the details of his laborious and ceremonial transition. I woke up Friday morning a wreck, which would have been fine except I had a 9am business meeting. It was already after 8am and the tears were streaming down with no sign of subsiding. If anything the floodgates only seemed to be opening wider and wider. This wave of emotion would not be contained or calmed. It was a torrent ripping through me. The logical part of me was thinking, "This is bad timing- can't I do this a little bit later, like in a few hours? This is just terribly inconvenient." It was too late to cancel and I was starting to panic which only made the emotional storm more pronounced. How was I going to put make-up on with tears pouring down my face? I had to surrender.

I grabbed a bunch of crystals and lay down on the bed. I had moonstones in my hands and pink tourmaline on my heart. As I wept, I prayed. I prayed to Goddess, God, Angels, Guardians, Guides and Grandpa. I cried out, "I need help. I can't do this by myself. Please help me." All of a sudden my breath involuntarily changed to a deeply energetic, loud fire breath. As this breath took over, a giant red fleshy eye in my heart chakra opened wide as currents of electric divine love coursed down from heaven above into the eye. My forearms began to vibrate and I could not move them. I felt the tears running down my cheeks as a feeling of profound peace and inner strength washed over me. In this instant everything changed. My prayers were answered completely. Divine peace bubbled up inside me, picked me up and carried me through the morning. I was able to pull myself together very quickly and I thought the business meeting went incredibly well. My heart felt pure, open and strong. Grief and prayer together held this secret key. Pain, loss and suffering can create pathways for the Divine to touch us, to hold us and to heal us.

The Teacher

Fifteen days after my grandfather passed away I dreamt of a dead owl. I held its sacred corpse delicately in my hands, divining with it, the feathers, the body. I ate part of the owl in a ritual, a somber ceremony of transubstantiation. I sacrificed myself to become the owl, seeking an occult lineage; an arcane transmission through ingestion of the owl. A teacher was there encouraging me from the shadows. A male teacher, yet no longer a man. I couldn't see him but I could sense him, except sometimes I saw his hands, a Shaman's hands.

It was a rite of passage. I was changed by the death of my grandfather, by understanding his absence. I was changed by assimilating his death and a piece of his spirit into myself, as I assimilated the owl. I stepped into the profound dark richness of the beckoning underworld. The owl is a doorway through which I pass.

As one generation falls away the next must rise into a new role. My grandfather was a fisherman. It was his hands that would catch the fish and kill it, clean it and cook it, to feed all his many progeny. It was his hands that endlessly transfigured life into death, into life again. It was his hands that held five babies and ten grandbabies. It was he who brought forth like a Magician, a Creator-Destroyer.

The time has come for my generation to catch and kill the fish, to clean it and cook it. Now we will carry the weight, as my grandfather did. My teacher was there to guide me through the symbolic owl door, to help me become the one who delicately and reverently holds Death in her hands and understands what it means; no longer an Owlet, but now an Owl.

CHAPTER SIXTEEN

The Eternal Threshold of Initiation

Imagine, if you will, the small circles of the moon dancing around the earth inside the larger coils of the sun, as Time slithers forward endlessly swallowing itself: years, seasons, days and nights, high tides and low. Every ending flowing into a beginning, the circle goes unbroken. Within this great clockworks of Time is your greatest power to change the future-the Present. The present links both the past and the future. You can create the future by the way you believe and behave in the present, using what you've learned from the past. The Fool of the Tarot reminds us that every single day is a new beginning. Every morning we are initiated again, stepping over the threshold to another sunrise, reborn.

The Fool represents the Spirit upon an earthly flight. He reminds us of our own Divinity and Unity. Any sense of duality is false- cosmic illusion. The Fool tells us that our lightness of heart and innocent faith will carry us through and enable us to laugh at all the cosmic jokes. Laughter is the proof of our faith. Our ability to transcend the darkness of mortality and accept the triumphs of the Devourer is a testament to our spiritual attainment. We are not distracted by the weight of the past or fear of the future so that we may focus our power to act in the present.

The Fool's number is zero, because we can always go back to zero, we can always begin again, we can always bring Humor and Faith to refresh our world view. The Fool reminds us that all that matters is the present, who we are today, how we think, what we do- right now. Instead of perceiving death and destruction in the world with morbidity and confusion, we can accept that one way or another, Time devours all. Yes, we are in on that joke. We get it. So, now is the time to do what we came to do. It's possible even, that as one cycle gives way to another we are leaving an age of darkness and entering one of lightness.

The Power of Right Now

Right now we are solidly within the New Age of Aquarius. We have passed through the great shift of 2012 according to the Mayan calendar. Also the Kali Yuga, The Dark Age is shifting into an Age of Truth known as Satya Yuga. While there is not a confirmed date for this shift it is said that the shift will be heralded by destruction, wars, tempestuous weather, floods and earthquakes. They say there will be a great upheaval as the earth shudders, whips up chaos and swallows civilizations. A new age begins, growing up from the wreckage- an age of illumination. And this too is part of the cosmic joke. If we can laugh at our own fate, we transcend it. Even when the world seems to be ending, know that it is just the beginning.

Perhaps it is true that the disorder in the world is a sign of the shifting of ages. Just as the Dark Age is at its apex of Death and Destruction, it is waning, as the seeds of the New Age were planted long ago and have been slowly, quietly sprouting. Do not be discouraged by Chaos, after all, it is the sacred stuff out of which Gaia formed herself. Focus on the blossoming of consciousness all around you. Connect with the Goddess and do what is in your power to change the future for the better. The wonderful thing about this new age is that it becomes astrologically more tenable for us to raise our spiritual vibrations. It is becoming easier to be illuminated. The veil is thinning and many channels are opening within you.

Go with Goddess

Like the serpent who bites her own tail, may the ending of this book be the beginning of something new. As you spiral forth, may you continue writing the story of your own sacred life. May the systems laid out in these pages inform you, as you choose your ways of being in the world. Your life is a beautiful dream of your soul's creation. Yours is an inviolate spirit upon an earthly flight; to be cherished, protected and nurtured by the Goddess. Allow her to hold you. Accept your own worthiness of such spiritual Unity and support, always.

As you move forward on your spiritual journey, there will be many points of departure as you follow the road of fulfillment and enlightenment. As you seek, you shall find. Just as this book found its way into your hands, so will other bodies of knowledge, signs of encouragement and path markers appear to you. As you merge with the Goddess, may She bless you, beyond your wildest dreams.

Cup your Hands Ritual

Wherever you are, whatever the season, whatever the weather, go outside. In the country, in the city, at work or at home- go outside. Cup your hands together in front of your heart. Extend your hands out as far as your arms will go to receive Nature. Let Nature fill your cup with rain, sunshine, snowflakes, wind, dead leaves, moonlight, darkness- whatever is in the air, right now. Close your hands and pull them in close to your heart. Cherish the moment. Give thanks for the blessings of the day, the night, the season. You are anointed, Priestess.

Lunar Flower Power Invocation

Speak these words aloud Sweet Sister:

"Embracing the Goddess within and inviting the union of Heaven and Earth within my vessel, I am in love with the Divine, which is all around me and within me. For spiritual gifts, healing, protection and guidance, I am grateful. I am faithful. I open and become the mystical channel. Through communion I am fulfilled in my blessed nature. I celebrate the earth, the moon, the stars, the sun, the wheel of the year, the rhythms of nature, life, death and rebirth. In this garden each aspect of life is sanctified. I wield the transformative power of ritual, the intentional act of blessing and the pure impulse which is transmitted through prayer. I am the earthly manifestation of the Goddess. I am a Lunar Flower."

ACKNOWLEDGMENTS

Thank you Tim for your constant love and support. Thank you Mom, Dad, Nina, Kate and all of the other Readers who so kindly and gently held and guided this project. Thank you Nicole for patiently delivering me to a place of faith and showing me the light over and over again. Thank you to all of the other Healers, Teachers and Friends along the way who fed my soul. Thank you Larry. Thank you Vivian. Thank you Misty. Thank you Star People. Thank you Ancestors. Thank you Nature Spirits. Thank you Goddess, God, Angels, Guardians and Guides.

DISCLAIMER

This book is for your inspiration only. It is not meant to take the place of professional healers, teachers and health care providers. Please use your great power of discernment, self-awareness and common-sense to know when to seek guidance and treatment from a trusted professional. The author does not accept responsibility for any outcomes or inspirations which may occur while reading this book.